THE 50-MILE RULE

THE 50-MILE RULE

Your Guide to Infidelity and Extramarital Etiquette

JUDITH E. BRANDT

TEN SPEED PRESS
Berkeley / Toronto

Ten Speed Press
P.O. Box 7123
Berkeley, California 94707
www.tenspeed.com

Distributed in Australia by Simon and Schuster Australia, in Canada by Ten Speed Press Canada, in New Zealand by Southern Publishers Group, in South Africa by Real Books, in Southeast Asia by Berkeley Books, and in the United Kingdom and Europe by Airlift Book Company.

Cover and Interior Design by Susan Van Horn

Library of Congress Cataloging-in-Publication Data

Brandt, Judith (Judith E.)
  The 50-mile rule : your guide to infidelity and extramarital
etiquette / by Judith Brandt.
      p. cm.
Includes bibliographical references and index.
  ISBN 1-58008-414-1
  1. Adultery. I. Title: Fifty-mile rule. II. Title.
  HQ806 .B73 2002
  306.73'6--dc21

2001008226

First printing, 2002

Printed in Canada

1 2 3 4 5 6 7 8 9 10 — 05 04 03 02 01

To Dorothy, above all.

CONTENTS

INTRODUCTION

This is a little book about affairs—why you want them and how to start, manage, and end them in a time when personal privacy is hard to find and even harder to maintain. For many people—perhaps your spouse—even the intimation of an affair constitutes a heinous crime. Affairs are forbidden fruit—the delights transitory, the consequences certain to be grisly.

Well, that's one opinion. So far as we're concerned, contemplating or even having an affair does not necessarily make you a bad person, an immoral person, a horny bastard, a shitheel, a slut, or any of the other colorful phrases that have been thrown at people who often just want a change of pace or some excitement or happiness in their lives. It just makes you human.

Affairs—a sexually intimate relationship between a married person and someone other than his or her spouse—have occurred in every culture and country since men and women started pairing up, lo, those many centuries ago, often in defiance of law, custom, religious edict, and yes, prior claim and affection.

It's estimated that at least half of all married men—and women—have cheated on their lawfully wedded spouses at least once at some point during their marriages, and sometimes a lot more than that. Sexual fidelity may be the standard by which marriages are measured, but it's a shaky standard indeed.

Given the possible consequences of infidelity, why do reasonable, rational adults risk their families, their homes, their lifestyle, and sometimes even their health, just to get a little something-something on the side?

Well, for every solid, life-enhancing marriage, there are probably three that are anything but. And where in the annals of human intercourse—no pun intended—exists a contract so rigid, so one-sided, and so frankly absurd in all its parts as the marriage contract?

Imagine owning a business and being confronted with a contract that:

◆ Restricted your company to using one vendor exclusively in perpetuity, even if quality and service diminish or disappear altogether;

◆ Made you legally and financially responsible for every act—good or bad—that occurred during the length of the contract;

◆ Baldly stated that, should the contract be dissolved, 50 percent—or more—of your personal and company assets could be assigned to the rejected vendor, also in perpetuity.

You'd tell the jerk sales guy to take a hike, right? No wonder they call marriage an institution—you should probably be committed for buying into it. And yet you probably stood up with at least a modicum of enthusiasm in front of a half-drunk crowd of relatives and friends and accepted exactly those same terms at your wedding, making a promise to have and hold and reject all others for thirty, forty, or fifty years—a lifetime. *Your* lifetime.

Dope. Oh well, who knew? Almost every marriage starts with absurdly high hopes fueled by that most potent of all mistresses, infatuation. Too bad the exciting and stimulating portion of the program usually dribbles to a halt, to be replaced all too soon by the realization that it may be time to move on, often when it's impossible to do so.

Let's face it—unless you have zero self-esteem or are just plain odd, you don't want to have sex with the same person forever and ever, you just don't.

But here you are, four or five years down the road from that fateful day when you vowed to forsake all others, etc. You're stuck with a mortgage, maybe a kid or two, and the awful realization that you could probably be doing a hell of a lot better than you are in the love and romance department. In other words, you're asking yourself:

- ◆ Why the hummer you got on the night before the wedding was the last she deigned to give;

- ◆ Why those long, romantic walks on the beach with the man of your dreams morphed into college football marathons and farting contests with his nephews;

◆ Why she gained 50 pounds and chopped her luscious long hair into that infernal "mommy cut;"

And, of course, the ever-popular,

◆ Why your adult life appears to be stretching out as an endless, barren void, years of sheer boredom punctuated by moments of utter contempt?

Well, you *are* asking, right?

A marriage can be described in many ways, but "easy" and "fair" are generally not part of the vocabulary. Both men and women get screwed in marriages all the time—screwed out of money, out of youth, out of joy, out of the simple pleasures we all dreamed that "partnership" would bring.

Of course, few people enter marriage thinking that boredom, if not complete calcification, is going to be the result. However, just as the urge to pair up is natural, so all too often is the urge to break apart when the initial excitement wears off and reality sets in. Some lucky people never feel that breakup urge. Others resist it and remain faithful and married, happily or not. Some divorce, perhaps to remarry again (and again and again in some cases).

Still others take a fourth route. They cheat.

The desire to periodically seek out new sexual and emotional relationships springs from a remarkably complex combination of factors, some biological, some chemical, some situational, some psychological. Contrary to the "till death do us part" contingent, nature and circumstance often conspire to put stringent time limits on marriage that can be difficult or impossible to override.

There seems to be within humans an "instinctive tug" toward infidelity—as opposed to one man/one woman and the sexual fidelity it implies—but no one really knows what kind of social and reproductive systems "man, unadorned" (or woman, for that matter) would adopt if society were suddenly stripped of experience, history, environment, and culture. Hard as it might be to believe when you're trapped within it, monogamy exists for any number of reasons, some of them actually good ones. Primary among them is the care of offspring.

Ah, children, the little devils . . . brought into the world not only to show your love—assuming there was any—for the partner that helped create them, but also to carry your genetic banner unto the next generation. Their creation and nurturing is at the heart of marriage—and adultery.

One of the essential differences between males and females is their relative fertility. Sperm is reasonably easy—and cheap—to produce, so males produce a lot of it and aren't loathe to spread it around. Eggs, on the other hand, are a lot harder to come by, making them far more valuable.

This is why in general terms men seek sex and women seek resources. Sex is the most popular and least clinical way to make those genetic flag-waving little tykes, and while rational men don't really set out to impregnate any and every woman who'll give them a tumble—too expensive for one thing—they're driven to find multiple mating opportunities as if they were.

Women, on the other hand, are driven to find the highest quality genes their looks can attract, along with the resources to raise the resulting children, if any, in style—and sometimes, one man just ain't the complete package. Hence, multiple mating may have benefits for women as well.

This is why, marriage vows notwithstanding, men often have only a short-term interest in relationships, while women, by necessity, are in it for the long haul, often looking to trade up quality- and resource-wise—despite the societal pressures exhorting them to stay together through thick and thin.

In other words, based on their varying reproductive and emotional needs, men and women are looking for very different things in marriage, differences that are often impossible to reconcile within a monogamous framework.

Yet, by design, marriages are much tougher to end than they are to enter into. Many people can't afford—or really don't want—to divorce. After all, even a rotten marriage can offer certain material, psychic, or social comforts you'd just as soon not be without.

Enter affairs, which offer both men and women the chance to

pursue tactical short-term sexual and emotional agendas while strategically maintaining the long-term socially monogamous relationship on which they may be emotionally, financially, and genetically dependent. Discreetly pursued, affairs can enhance or at least prolong marriages, by way of venting frustration or refocusing pent-up sexual or emotional hunger.

Hence this handy guide. Read *The 50-Mile Rule* to discover . . .

◆ What led you to marry in the first place, and why you're now having second—and third—thoughts about it;

◆ The difference between social and sexual monogamy, and why society's strict marriage restrictions might not be working for you;

◆ How to choose likely affair partners, where to conduct your trysts, and how to keep your secret life a secret;

◆ How affairs differ in length and intensity, and how to manage them;

◆ Strategies for ending affairs with a minimum of muss and fuss;

◆ What to do if you're found out—and the consequences for telling the truth. (Hint: don't.)

From the self-explanatory Rule #1 of affairs (don't get caught) to the 50-Mile Rule (spouse and lover should never live within fifty miles of each other) and beyond, I'll show you how to maximize your options while minimizing risk (no guarantees, of course).

There's nothing inherently immoral about seeking additional or even primary sexual or emotional fulfillment outside of marriage if keeping a socially monogamous relationship together will benefit you—or your existing kids. After all, what's better—to walk away from them in frustration, or to quietly deal with your personal needs elsewhere while maintaining the secure home life so vital to giving them a good start in life?

Of course, you don't need kids as a reason to stay married, yet many a spouse involved in a childless marriage has strayed on occasion, and why not? Affairs can supplement marriages and help keep existing relationships fresh. They're not always a substitute by any means. In trying to maintain social and sexual bonds consisting of one man and one woman forever and ever, we're going against some of biology's most deep-seated inclinations.

Even so, monogamy remains the standard by which Western civilization measures morality. Revealed affairs *do* hurt other people, often the people you mean to hurt least. Just because our bodies and emotions and brains (wherever they may be located) sometimes impel us to act in certain ways doesn't make the possible fallout any less real or painful. The desire to cheat may be part of nature's Big Game—its version of a Bronx cheer—but it's not a competition for the naïve, squeamish, or careless. An affair can generate ugly and painful consequences, whether it's discovered or not. It can ruin your life as easily as improve it, sometimes simultaneously.

None of which, by the way, has to do with guilt, which is a societal construct specifically designed to keep you in line, a feeling you'll learn to ignore with practice. What really makes an affair right or wrong is the way you handle your ongoing responsibilities—to your spouse, your lovers, and your children. Treating your family badly is wrong. Treating yourself to a little extramarital R&R could be oh-so-very-right. Who decides? *You do.*

PART I

WEDLOCK, A PADLOCK

THE THREE KINDS OF SEX

House sex: when you're newly married and have sex all over the house in every room.

Bedroom sex: after you've been married for a while, you just have sex in the bedroom.

Hall sex: after you've been married for a while longer, you just pass each other in the hall and say, "Fuck you."

CHAPTER 1

Your Cheatin' Heart

A very wise person once compared cheating on your spouse to cheating on income taxes: most people do but rarely admit it; those who don't wish they had the guts to do so; and everyone cautions their children against it, but fully expects the advice to be ignored.

These days marital infidelity is the rule rather than the exception. Sexual exclusivity in marriage often comes about more from exhaustion and fear of consequences than it does from a genuine desire to restrict sexual and emotional relations to a single person as long as you both shall live. Given the right person and the right circumstances, many people will eventually succumb to the desire to cheat, whatever their vows to the contrary.

The fact that affairs happen doesn't exactly warrant a news-flash in this day and age. Even so, it's safe to assume that most people marry fully expecting that they'll be faithful in every way to their partners for a lifetime . . . till reality sets in.

After all, a whole mythology has evolved around marriage. Just look at the obscene amounts of money and ridiculous lengths to which some people go to make their wedding day "special," often bankrupting themselves (or their parents) in the process. Even cynics impart magical powers to this union, this Event, after which joined lives supposedly take on a particularly lustrous tinge.

Well, maybe. After all, the need to love and be loved is inherent in the human animal. We need, crave, demand affection. We want continual recognition for those qualities—good and bad—that combine to make us unique. It's these emotional needs among others that lead us to legally merge with other people. But these mergers have consequences that society must control.

Somehow marriage, initially a simple offspring-for-protection contract, became a sacrament, a marvelous and mysterious vessel into which two people mix their wishes, fears, and dreams in the fervent hope that the resulting concoction will remain bubbly and sustain them for the next—gasp—fifty years or more.

Well, it works that way for some people, those lucky couples that seem "made for each other," who remain unfazed at the bumps in the road that cause the rest of us to crash and burn. And, according to romance novels and magazines and the chattering classes, if your relationship falls short, if *you* are unable to achieve total joy and happiness, emotional and sexual fidelity, and intimacy decade after decade by way of a marital commitment you might've made in your teens or twenties, if *you* resent the opportunity cost inherent in staying with a person who no longer suits you, then the fault lies not in your stars— but in you.

Baloney.

A successful marriage entails hard work and a continual willingness to compromise. It starts with good raw materials—generally two compatible people with similar goals and interests who use those heady initial sensations of infatuation and romantic love as a base for further personal and interdependent growth. And it helps if these individuals were not compromise choices, but the best that either could ever make.

Romantic love, as we'll see, is in many ways a chemical reaction on a timetable, one prompted by your body's desire to mate and reproduce with a particular person who has general characteristics that you like—characteristics, by the way, that dozens or hundreds of other people whom you haven't even met, might share.

Being in love is truly a wondrous process, and when people fall, the need and desire to be connected takes precedence over everything else. But the chemicals

> ### FUN ADULTERY FACT
>
> Monogamy means having a male and female who are both social and reproductive partners. It only implies, but doesn't guarantee, sexual fidelity. There can be a world of difference between social and sexual monogamy.

that spur togetherness generally wear off in four or five years, and when they do, what's called "mature love" (oh, the horrors that phrase implies) is supposed to take over.

Mature love entails ongoing respect, mutual affection, and commitment. Feel this for your spouse and you'll probably stay married—in other words, socially and maybe even sexually monogamous. If not, all that may be left is a tangled, exhausting web of financial and family commitments, prior history, and the vestiges of a relationship that doesn't mean what it used to. Even within a happy, evolving marriage, you may still be driven to find supplemental sex and passion in the form of seductive new options.

Why? Well, in part, there's ancient programming at work, deeply imbedded in your genes (segments of DNA that tell cells how to function). These programs have been handed down over hundreds of successful couplings by your ancestors, and may be driving you to unconsciously explore the myriad of other reproductive options out there (unless, of course, you choose not to).

At the same time, technology has allowed us to pursue sex without undue concern about replicating every time we "do it." While humans have almost certainly evolved with what are called "reproductive–relevant tendencies," sex has value beyond reproduction alone. It can be both relational (meaning that we use it to enhance and give resonance to relationships) and recreational (meaning

A FEW WORDS ABOUT UNCONSCIOUS DRIVES . . .

Humans are indeed driven by more than just biology. Culture, environment, upbringing, traumatic events, etc. all influence our decisions and choices over time. There are many things that we choose consciously to make happen—or not—and with full consideration of the consequences.

There are, however, also functions over which we have no conscious control. Breathing, electrical impulses in the brain, muscle movement—these are activities that occur without our specific awareness, effort, or direction. And there is growing scientific evidence that the process of falling in love—or lust—works in just the same way. Through a mysterious process that is only now yielding its secrets to science, our bodies may very well "choose" with whom to fall in love without our conscious consent.

Even so, though we may not be able to control our innate desires, we can manage them and make decisions based on more than instinct and desire. Consciousness and choice are gifts for which we should all be grateful, whether we utilize them fully or not. To live a life in thrall to your most basic urges would be to live an ugly life indeed.

that it's a hell of way to spend a chilly afternoon—or a hot one for that matter). And even if those needs are being met in your primary relationship, you just might want more of a good thing.

After all, marriage is a social contract, a way to assign responsibility for children and the transfer of property. Social contracts can be a roadblock when it comes to acting on other impulses, but it can't actually stop them, which is why moral and legal sanctions generally aren't worth diddly when it comes to cheating.

And while kids and property are indeed important, it's a little much to conclude that a ridiculously one-sided contract that you entered into when you were young and stupid should end up eliminating all your other genetic and romantic options for the rest of time.

Nevertheless, marriage has become so drenched with moral and financial significance that it's no surprise that people tend to get hysterical when they suspect that an outside party—such as your new lover—is trying to horn in on the action. Which is where the busybody industry comes in.

Go into any bookstore and check out the "relationship" section, or listen to talk show "love doctors" and you'll hear the same mantra over and over again: men who cheat on their wives are immature and can't handle responsibility, they had lousy childhoods, they're bored, vengeful, and pissed off that the wife has gotten fat and is obsessing about the kids. They're afraid of intimacy, phobic about commitment, and/or are in the middle of a midlife crisis.

Women are supposed to have a moral purity about them that precludes them from seeking a little on the side. Why then do so many of them "step out" on their husbands? Try loneliness, boredom, emotional torment. Their husbands stink in bed (literally and figuratively) and ignore them. The kids grow up, Mom hits the wall, and suddenly there's a "love void" the husband refuses to fill.

Are these logical reasons to seek sex and affection outside of marriage? On the surface, sure. Emotional and psychological needs all by themselves can create a pretty awful tangle when it comes to relationships between the sexes, not to mention finances and the pressure that comes from living in close proximity to anyone for an extended length of time.

But in general, things like commitment phobia and immaturity are just sideshows to the unconscious drive to perpetuate ourselves through genetic variety and access to better resources and better genes. We experience feelings and emotions toward other people when our bodies want us to take certain actions to certain ends. And to our bodies, there's no more important action than that which may lead to reproduction—sex, in other words—no matter who else we may be legally bound to.

Still, the "helping professions" often look at emotions and feelings as things apart from and unrelated to biological functions. Why? Because the very idea that the body might try mightily to kick the mind into gear just to satisfy its most base reproductive needs is politically incorrect in the extreme.

Even less PC is the theory that love not only takes different forms based on your gender, but that it can be finite, situational, and even predatory, a chemical reaction preprogrammed to self-destruct, often on a timetable that doesn't jibe with that of the spouse who may be left holding the diaper bag or mortgage payment book.

Pretty painful concepts, huh? The drives that incite so many people to marry, mate, cheat, or divorce, and start over again in pursuit of a possibly better genetic outcome may be an integral part of the human reproductive pattern, and may exist for good reasons in the aggregate, but they certainly create great anguish among humans individually. Such patterns aren't conducive to modern life, with its two-income families, huge financial commitments, and children often requiring help long past their teenage years. We may be living in the space age, but our internal programming remains strictly stone age.

This is why society has created laws and cultural norms to keep us in line so that we'll fulfill our contracted responsibilities toward both children and spouses. Yet even though science has managed to curb the tendency of sex to lead almost inevitably to reproduction, the reproductive imperatives that have been coded into our DNA are still highly motivating factors, dictating in many ways the conscious choices we make each day about dating, marriage, and beyond.

Let's see how this works in practice for singles—and for marrieds.

CHAPTER 2

LOVE IS A BATTLEFIELD

*M*eet Tanya and Bob. Tanya's in her mid-twenties, a nice person with an average education and average looks that she hasn't done much to improve. Her life is pretty boring in fact, without much opportunity for interaction with the other sex, so when Bob, a new vendor for her company, asks her out, she's utterly thrilled.

Bob's a nice enough guy, also single, the salesman type who dresses well and always gives off an air of knowing what's what. They go on their date to a reasonably pleasant restaurant near a big mall— not quite The Plaza, but a distinct improvement over Tanya's usual Budget Gourmet repast. By the time the small talk's over and the entrées arrive, Tanya's smitten and has already picked out the china pattern, the kids' names, and the neighborhood in which she and the lucky bridegroom will reside.

Bob, on the other hand, is already bored to death with Tanya's incessant chatter about her company and her cat and the art courses she's taking at the local college. His main concern is wondering what she looks like with her clothes off, period. Like most guys, he won't bother paying any attention to what she says till he's slept with her, and often not even then. He'll put up with her yakking long enough to maybe get laid, but even if she does put out, he'll never call again either way, no matter how long Tanya waits for the phone to ring.

A common enough scenario, open to the usual interpretations—he's a user, she's immature—men just want one thing, and women want everything, right?

Well, right, and why not? Bob is out for the quick lay because for millions of years it's been to the man's advantage to hit and run—to try and create as many children as possible, for as little parental investment as possible. Men are highly sexed because, as we mentioned earlier, they're highly fertile. Since sperm is reasonably easy—and cheap—to produce, Bob doesn't mind sharing it with just about any woman who meets his basic criteria and is amenable to the offer, even though he consciously wants nothing to do with kids right now, his or anyone else's. He's not even aware of the underlying reproductive rationale behind his desire to bed anything that moves that isn't too skanky.

Just what is that rationale? On the most basic level, putting aside those annoying moral aspects for a moment, the more women Bob can impregnate and skip out on without financial penalty, the better his handhold on the next generation. Different kids by different mothers have different traits, and who knows which traits will be required for future success? Bob will "bond"—and perhaps offer marriage and resources—only with those women whom his body considers the very best long-term bet. Tanya's someone that Bob will have sex with, sure, but reproductively she doesn't make the cut.

Eggs, on the other hand, are relatively scarce, which is why women try to be far more choosy about their bedmates if they can. Yet Tanya doesn't date much, so Bob's attention is not only a treat, but a rare opportunity to fulfill her own unconscious reproductive needs. No wonder she's desperate to make him like her—it may be her only chance for marriage and a family. And in this society married people have status—hence her wedding daydreams.

Should Tanya get pregnant by Bob, she'll need all of his resources in order to raise the child who may be her sole genetic legacy, resources he'll part with only if he bonds with her. Which is where her desperate and vaguely pathetic invitation for closeness comes from. She's trying to make him like her via the barrage of nervous chatter he can't stand.

Keep in mind that all this reproductive byplay is strictly under the radar. As we mentioned before, in our society sex has more than just reproductive value. It's fun and is something that many people want more of just for that reason. Not every coupling takes place because one or both of the parties involved have a burning, conscious interest in creating children. Nevertheless, the emotions Bob and Tanya feel and the direction their date is taking are very much influenced by the imperatives of the human mating system.

As for Tanya, well, she'll probably give in to Bob all right—who knows when another guy will happen along? Still, the gates will open only after Bob has demonstrated access to resources (by paying for dinner). If he wants sex, he must also demonstrate an ability to get through her defenses. To do that, he has to at least go through the motions of getting to know her a little. She will translate this minor time investment into genuine interest on Bob's part, which is why she'll end up waiting weeks for a call that's never going to come, even if she does sleep with him.

Of course, there are plenty of other influences at play here. If Tanya does get pregnant, perhaps Bob will marry her, from guilt or family pressure or his own sense of morality. Civil laws and edicts have evolved over time to deal with just these sorts of issues (although not very effectively), and DNA tests have made it that much tougher for guys to skip out on their responsibilities—or for women to cuckold men into raising kids they didn't father for that matter.

But the reproductive pressures pushing the unmarried Bob and Tanya apply to married people too. The real difference is that our unmarried lovers have only minimal legal claims on each other, and virtually no prior claim. They're free agents, which married men and women most assuredly are not.

Let's turn, now, to Tom and Gloria. Tom, a reasonably happily married man, sees Gloria at a convention. She's gorgeous—something along the lines of what his wife was two kids and thirty pounds ago. He's turned on. They have a drink. He's excited, she's available—they have sex, a coupling so raucous and delightful that Tom's actually glad to get home, though for the next few weeks his dreams are filled with this mystery woman. Eventually he goes back to his old routine and forgets about her, guilt-free because he didn't get caught.

Why did he do it? A therapist could pull out all sorts of motives—boredom, simmering aggravation with his wife and the kids, repressed anger at his parents' divorce. Surely he must have known the very real downside of having spontaneous sex with an unknown woman—disease, discovery, harassment, pregnancy—yet he fell just the same, marriage vows be damned.

But now that we know that temptation is to a large degree the body's way of encouraging the actions that might ensure better reproductive outcomes, Tom's motivations become clearer. Perhaps his wife was a true compromise choice—the best he could do at the time, but no great shakes. Even his kids are a little disappointing, despite the investment he's made in them. Enter Gloria—vivacious, seductive, no-maintenance, and, driven by her own agenda, interested. In taking her to bed, Tom was responding to a reproductive "call of the wild" that could certainly have been thwarted but not denied.

What was Gloria's agenda? Well, she might just want some recreational sex after a tough day. Or, at some level she's not even aware of, she might want another baby, but one different from the son that's turning out a little too much like his father. So for her, sex with Tom was a chance to collect some sperm from a man with appealing genetics despite no potential as a long-term social partner. Then she went home, had sex with her husband for possible cover, and voilà, gave birth nine months later to a baby girl that her husband was thrilled to call his own, since Gloria gave him no reason to think otherwise.

> **FUN ADULTERY FACT**
>
> "Mommy's babies, daddy's maybes"—an estimated 10% of all children conceived within marital relationships are in fact not genetically related to the legal father.

Now, Gloria's pursuing a risky strategy indeed by tricking her husband into raising the little girl. These days even a routine blood test could show that he's not the father.

Let's assume, however, that he doesn't find out. Who then is the winner in this little scenario? Well, Tom gets a bonus baby that he doesn't need to support, who may end up being his only genetic legacy if something happens to his legitimate kids; Gloria gets a child with traits she likes better; and Tom's wife knows nothing about any of it. So all are winners.

The only out-and-out loser is Gloria's husband, who's being

screwed financially and maybe genetically too if something happens to his biological son and only child. Obviously Gloria should really divorce him and give him a chance to have more kids and perhaps find permanence with someone else, but he's a good long-term provider who will give the children a fine home and it's hard to find paternally minded men these days. Given the choice, she'll take her genetic legacy over her husband's any day.

A FEW WORDS ABOUT PARENTAL INVESTMENT . . .

In a genuine research breakthrough with big implications for under-standing human interactions, a prominent biologist has demonstrated that a key element in male/female differences comes from the notion of parental investment. This can be defined as anything having value or cost—time or energy, for example—that a parent endures on behalf of children and that increases the likelihood that they will be successful, often at the cost of directing those same resources toward some other, possibly more productive offspring. Eggs are big investments, so parental investment on the part of women is generally high. Sperm are not big investments, so male paternal investment is often relatively low.

To find a guy who not only wants kids but is willing to help raise them is a coup indeed. That's why women generally stay with good providers, even if they've sought out other genetic fathers for their kids—and why some men run the risk of raising children not their own.

A callous attitude? Well, duh. But on some level Gloria's body judged that the possible reproductive benefits of infidelity outweighed the risk. So did Tom. Their bodies then generated emotions and feelings that drove them to mate outside of their primary relationships. Very attracted to each other, they ignored everything they ever learned about the sanctity of the marriage bed and acted on their unspoken—and on a conscious level, unfathomable—desire to maybe improve their genetic handhold on the next generation.

Can't this programming be overridden? Of course, by way of the personal behaviors we call "free will." (It's these behaviors, in fact, that therapists tinker with.) Choose not to hit the override button, however, and you could be on your way to an affair.

Rationally speaking, creating a child with an illicit lover is the last thing on earth most people want to do. (After all, when it comes to divorce or paternity suits, kids are the gifts that keep on giving, an annuity for the custodial parent.) But we already know that rationality doesn't always figure into the equation. Suppose, for example, that you're infertile. Surely this makes you an unlikely candidate for an affair, if having kids is the subliminal goal, right?

On the contrary. According to one controversial theory, if infertility's the issue, it could just take sex with the right person—someone other than your spouse in this case—to create a happy reproductive outcome where none existed in your marriage. In other words, infertility may sometimes be situational, an unconscious defense mechanism designed to keep you from being burdened with genetically inferior children.

And if that's the case, there may be a real benefit to going outside your marriage for viable genes—shucking off sexual monogamy—while retaining the primary socially monogamous relationship upon which that child might be dependent.

A FEW WORDS ABOUT SPERM COMPETITION . . .

The sperm competition theory posits the radical notion that, if a female engages in multiple matings with more than one male during a concentrated period of time, their sperm will actually "fight" for the right to fertilize the egg and may the best man win, so to speak. With the help of DNA fingerprinting, biologists are discovering that, within the animal kingdom at least, some females will mate with more than one male and unconsciously or intuitively direct the outcome of sperm competition to their liking (the winner being the male with the best genes), all the while gathering resources from all the males in return for sexual access.

Should this hold true for humans—and early indications are that it will—this theory, in conjunction with the notion of parental investment, has many implications for marital relationships. These theories taken together could explain a great deal about why some people can remain sexually faithful for a lifetime while others cannot—or choose not to.

So the drive for sex outside of marriage seems to have as much to do with the relentless beat of genetic variety and improvement as it does with each individual's search for lasting meaning and companionship. Marriage, however, still sings a siren song that holds most of us in thrall to its implied promise of sexual fidelity and love both deep and lasting.

Good luck.

CHAPTER 3

LOVE IS THE DRUG

*L*ove is a marvelous thing full of mystery, and a life full of love would be considered a success by most human standards. However, the measure of your *biological* success is the number of descendants you leave behind. The winners in the gene contest shape the future after all, and most people are programmed to try and win at this game to the best of their abilities.

That's why most people just love to have sex (and why women often lose interest after their kids are born). Thanks to free will, you can choose not to play, and a damn good thing too, since the body can interpret every potential reproductive tête-a-tête in a faulty light, destroying lives instead of enhancing them.

There are pros and cons to both sexual fidelity and infidelity. Fidelity generally comes out ahead when the issue is not rocking the marital boat. But from the standpoint of winning the gene game, neither fidelity nor infidelity is inevitably good or bad. What *is* bad is making mistakes—choosing the wrong spouse, cheating when you should have stayed faithful, remaining faithful to an inferior choice when you should have been screwing anything that moved. In other words, you've got to know when to hold 'em and when to fold 'em, which, given the tangle of emotions and physical drives and legalities, is often hard to do.

There are two major forces that influence our attraction to one another—psychological needs and physiological drives. These interact and overlap constantly, fluidly influencing and reinforcing our behaviors.

Physiological drives are what impel us to eat, breathe, and pro-create—the unconscious stuff, the basics. Psychological needs, on the other hand, are emotional and intellectual—higher level, conscious functions. Sure, your body can chemically induce feelings of sexual excitement in the hopes that you'll mate with someone new despite an existing spouse, but it's your personal belief system and your values that will either let you indulge yourself or stop you from doing so, whether from consideration, fear of discovery, or just timidity.

Sexual fidelity is tough to maintain not only because of the emotional wear and tear we suffer when in constant proximity to another person, but because the very chemicals that induced us to bond in the first place often have an expiration date. Once we iden-tify someone on some level as a likely candidate for love, a chemical process is activated. It starts with PEA, a molecule and natural amphetamine produced in the brain.

When the amount of PEA in the brain neurons goes up, it produces amazing feelings, that great "love high" you get when you come across a sexually desirable and potentially compatible individual. It induces all those feelings of dizzy, romantic love that we wish would last forever.

Well, they don't (and maybe that's a good thing). This crazy-making high can last for minutes, days, or months but rarely more than two to three years. When you're in a constant mental tizzy, it's hard to concentrate on anything beyond your new beloved, and so the brain finally reacts to this constant overstimulation (and the constant sex that often accompanies it, more's the pity) by sending in oxytocin, an endorphin produced in the pituitary gland. This is a calming agent that makes you feel connected while getting you back to somewhat normal feelings and reactions.

And once the endorphins march in, the romantic love portion of the program is over, at least so far as this particular mate is concerned. Instead, you feel attachment and contentment, a bond that seems to exist for a very specific reason—so that you'll stay in the relationship long enough

> **FUN ADULTERY FACT**
>
> *People who remain happily married over long periods of time have higher concentrations of endorphins.*

to see the child you may have produced through its toughest period, the first years of life.

But alas, most people produce fewer endorphins as time goes by, and the feelings of contentment and attachment fade. And when all the chemicals have worn off—usually after four or five years—what you may have left is nothing but a sense of neutrality, or disillusion, toward your spouse and the life you have built together, which also exists for a specific biological reason. If the original bond between you and your current mate has faded, and there's no longer a strong connection, then it's going to be that much easier for you to move on to new and different matings. It's as if your body perceives that your genetic success might be enhanced by new sexual pairings and wants to lower the psychological barriers to them by encouraging marital dissatisfaction.

So, thanks to the chemical nature of love and the psychological pull between bonding and seeking individuation, marriages have a life cycle that runs as follows:

◆ **INFATUATION**—someone you meet rocks your world, and romance is in the air.

◆ **ATTACHMENT**—you feel content and bonded just being around that person, but romantic love is over.

◆ **DISILLUSION**—the first cracks in the firmament of your overall relationship appear and often grow.

◆ **DISSOLUTION**—you bail.

Outside factors have an undeniable impact on the marriage life cycle too. If your spouse is a cheapskate or a drunk or a loser or a workaholic or just one of those people who seem to live under a perpetual black cloud, your marriage is going to be impacted in a big way.

Nevertheless, despite outside influences, this is pretty much a chemically induced timetable, one made all the more complicated by the fact that your spouse is running the table too, only at a different rate of speed, and one that may not jibe with yours. She or he may still be at the attachment stage when you're past ready to leave.

If romantic love has evolved into mature love, if you're compatible and affectionate toward each other and more or less on the same relationship timetable, chances are good that you'll be able to either bypass or work around the neutral feelings, staying married and maybe even faithful. In other words, you may never come to the dissolution stage.

After all, there may be a real genetic benefit in mating with this one person only and then making the parental investment necessary to raise the resulting kids the way you want to. In this situation, the costs of infidelity may be too great. If your spouse meets most of your needs, and your kids are the best you can realistically hope for, you don't want to risk losing them through divorce, and you certainly don't want a stepparent, evil or otherwise, raising them.

And much the same can hold true for childless marriages. Childless or not, if you're content in your choice overall, there's no particular reason to rock the boat by seeking out other sexual and emotional pairings that might not yield half the overall satisfaction. After all, one just doesn't "come across" a potential new mate or adultery partner every day. For some people, the risk of rejection or potential humiliation makes looking for a new partner something not worth undertaking.

A FEW WORDS ABOUT INFATUATION . . .

To be in romantic love is to be involved in one of the greatest of all human experiences. That wild, roller-coaster ride, those fabulous feelings of need and want and desire—what could be better? Chances are you felt just this way when fate directed you to your current spouse. In the beginning at least, you probably felt that you'd never, ever want to leave, that this person must truly be the culmination of your search and that you'll never feel that way about anyone ever again.

Were that the case, however, there'd be a lot fewer multiple marriages, and probably fewer affairs too. The reality is that, while infatuation for a new person can hit at any time, you only get one shot per person. In other words, once the romantic love stage of your marriage or relationship is over, you'll never be able to rekindle it with your spouse or lover to the same degree. The only way to get those marvelous feelings back full force is through a new relationship.

But let's say that the marriage has been a disappointment and that you just want out. The fact of the matter is that you're committed—possibly to a child, and maybe to a house and car and a host of other stuff you can't deal with on your own. Or you *do* meet someone with potentially earth-shattering implications for the rest of your life. What then?

Well, you've got some choices:

- You can chuck it all and go the serial monogamy route—get a divorce and possibly remarry.

- You can gut it out and stay faithful in an increasingly stale relationship—the calcification route, but boy, are you ever fulfilling your marriage vows!

- You can join a religious order and forgo sex forever.

- Or, you just concede that divorce isn't an option and cheat, maintaining the social monogamy upon which your livelihood, reputation, children, and resources may depend, while seeking out other more palatable sexual options.

Love is a drug, and, in the end, even genuine affection for your spouse and kids can't inoculate you against wanderlust and the urge to merge with someone else. So what on earth impelled you to marry in the first place, and how on earth did monogamy become not the exception but the rule?

CHAPTER 4

A BRIEF HISTORY OF MARRIAGE

*H*umans exist to reproduce. You're here on this planet to xerox yourself and as a result your body generates feelings and emotions—lust, infatuation, and sometimes attachment and even love—to encourage you to do so, even if on a conscious or physical level you can't have or don't want kids.

And it's to satisfy that basic reproductive drive that human beings have been pairing up since they started walking on two feet. The desire to meet, mate, and bond with the often temporary object of your affection has everything to do with nature's need to provide resources to any resulting children till they can somewhat fend for themselves.

Even among hunter-gatherers a loose form of monogamy seems to have existed, a man and a woman joined together more or less exclusively for reproductive purposes. But such unions didn't necessarily last for long, and not just because life spans were much shorter then.

Why? The answer's fertility, and it's one of the keys to understanding why marriages often run into trouble.

First, let's review. Men are, at least in theory, endlessly fertile. One man could conceivably have children with hundreds, if not thousands of women (assuming he had the stamina). On some level, it's in a man's best genetic interest to "hit and run" and have children by as many women as possible, while taking responsibility only for the best bets.

Women, on the other hand, can produce only a limited number of children, so every one counts. By necessity they look for the best providers, the best looking and most successful men they can attract. They want to snare not only the highest-quality genes but also the greatest number of resources.

And because it takes a long time to raise a child to be independent, women want a man who will stick around and help—a desire, you'll note, that's diametrically opposed to the way most men would operate if they had their druthers. Men and women aren't just from different planets—they're from different solar systems.

These differences in fertility mean that, in general, men and women take a very different path to the same destination—genetic survival.

For thousands of years people have courted, fallen in love, mated,

> **FUN ADULTERY FACT**
>
> *Men seek sex,
> women seek resources.*

and raised children, just like we do today. But because our ancestors weren't connected by legal or social bonds, once infatuation faded and the stress of day-to-day living set in, a "couple" could break up without much fuss, the better to find new genetic options.

Of course, life was more communal back then too, and leaving was easier. Men could wander off secure in the knowledge that the woman's extended family would help care for his progeny, often leaving women equally free to seek out a better partner with a bigger spear, perhaps a wandering hunter from another tribe.

This makes sense. A periodic, fresh infusion of genes prevents inbreeding and creates kids with different strengths and new traits, leading to a more varied talent pool. And different fathers, each with at least a temporary stake in seeing his child past the dangers of infancy, meant more resources for the group as a whole, and other benefits for the mother in particular.

Men and women most likely followed a "serial monogamy" pattern, changing partners numerous times during their reproductive years, staying reasonably (but not overly) faithful within each relationship. When they got disillusioned or bored with their current mate, when the kids could walk by themselves instead of being carried, the parents would split up.

As society became more complex and populous, the hunters settled down and joined the gatherers in villages. Growing populations meant close proximity and a need for orderly relationships. So customs evolved that defined "right" and "wrong" behaviors, religions came along to sanction those customs, and laws were created to codify and enforce the customs so that a majority of people adhered to them, ensuring social stability.

And once people started staying in one place, concepts like "ownership" and "property" came into being. And once certain people—virtually all men—began owning land and accumulating wealth, the next question became, how do I pass this property along, and to whom?

Well, who better than a son created of his own seed? But, of course, back in those days, a man could never really be sure that the children he supported were actually his. (Remember "mommy's babies, daddy's maybes"?) Women, in their own search for superior genes and resources, were even then perfectly capable of tricking men into raising kids conceived by others with better looks or better traits.

So it became vital to men that their mates remain "pure" and unsullied. That way, paternity could never be doubted. In return women received protection and economic resources. Marriage as a legal entity evolved in part so that men could better control women's sexuality, while transferring property in an orderly manner from one generation to the next. If the couple in question actually loved each other, so much the better. But love was hardly a requirement.

Men, of course, saw no particular need to control their own sexuality. After all, it was assumed for thousands of years that women were merely the vessel in which children grew, that they actually contributed nothing else to the party. Even if a woman were raped or otherwise forced to have sex against her will, it was considered not an infraction against her, but against her husband or father. As a general rule, only women were punished for adultery.

So where, precisely, did the concept of monogamy come into the picture? After all, as men began to acquire property, some managed to snag a lot more than others. Then as now, some guys are just smarter or better looking or luckier or meaner or greedier or just more likely to tap into the finer things in life. Like the song says, some guys get all the breaks. And based on what we now know about human sexual patterns, it only stands to reason that women would tend to gravitate to men with power and—here's that word again—resources, all the better to give their offspring a flying start at life (and themselves a better wardrobe).

And let's face it—guys with money or power don't have to be good looking or super-sexy to attract the cream of the female crop. It doesn't matter whether it's prehistoric times, medieval times, or today, resource-rich and successful men generally attract a crowd of good-looking women, all wanting their little piece of the action.

This may leave some pretty slim pickins for the average dude, assuming he can find a woman to hook up with at all. And this may provide part of the rationale behind what's referred to as Socially Imposed Monogamy (SIM) as it's practiced—and dreaded in some cases—in Western countries.

And a rationale is needed. If men in particular are mildly polygynous (one man, several women)—which research indicates they are—then why would the successful men, the guys who could attract lots of women, guys with power and authority, allow a "one man–one woman till death do us part" system to cut into what must have been a pretty sweet deal?

Theories abound. One holds that SIM is a way to get lower-ranking males involved in government and defense of property. After all, if a small number of high-ranking guys divide all the high-quality women among them, there's not likely to be much left over for the lower-ranking males, which could lead to insurrection.

Another theory holds that SIM became the "rule" because the Catholic Church and the aristocracy of the time were engaged in an enormous conflict, in which the Church fought mightily to impose its will over the secular authority of the wealthy classes. The control of reproduction—and inheritance—had major implications for the Church, since the more children a wealthy family had, the less wealth might be available to the Church when the patriarch of the family passed on.

Marriage and reproduction were key to one of the major political questions of the time: who rules—the spiritual or the temporal? If marital issues could be adjudicated by the Church alone, then the Church was in effect controlling reproduction, which is an overwhelmingly critical issue for many people with serious implications for their future. By making marriage and childbearing issues of profound spiritual gravity, the Church could bring the aristocracy to heel.

And since the Church had pretty negative views about sex (advocating marriage only because it was a way to control people's overwhelming sexual impulses), the grudging standard became one man/ one woman for life. In fear for their mortal souls, the aristocracy (just like the peasant down the street), gave in, and SIM became the norm.

Although the theories are fascinating, there's probably no single answer as to why SIM is the rule in most Western countries. We do know, however, that as mobility increased and religion loosened its hold, relinquishing its "all-knowing" role, husbands and wives had to take far more active roles in the spiritual and overall development of their families, relying on themselves, as opposed to the community at large, to ensure their kids' development.

In order to shoulder such heavy burdens, spouses had to start treating each other more like equal partners. And this being the case, it helped if the people involved were both companionable and compatible. The idea of marrying for love wasn't far behind.

But here's where the story takes another ironic twist. Parents stayed together because they were almost exclusively responsible for their kids' welfare and upbringing. At the same time, these children required more training than ever before in order to deal with an increasingly complex outside world.

So, the state-imposed aspect of monogamy aside, lifelong marriage actually did make some sense—at a time when the average person's reproductive life began at sixteen or eighteen, and the average life expectancy was maybe forty years old.

Fast-forward to the twenty-first century. Life expectancies of seventy, eighty, or even ninety years are now relatively common, but we are still admonished to keep marriages that might last a half-century or more intact and sexually exclusive long after the kids are gone—a vaguely depressing prospect to say the least.

And yet, here we are. For many people (probably your spouse), marriage remains a sacrament, and sexual fidelity within it a foregone conclusion, if an unlikely one.

This brings us to the next point—why you chose your particular spouse. Picking a long-term mate is among the most important decisions you'll ever make. This only makes more absurd the fact that, with all our freedom these days to try before we buy, so many people choose so badly.

CHAPTER 5

CHOOSING SPOUSES— AND LOVERS

*E*ven today, with divorce relatively common, legal entanglements alone make marriage something to approach with caution. Nevertheless, people marry every day. But there are hundreds, if not thousands, of prospective mates out there with similar characteristics. Why is it that one candidate turns us on, while a similar one leaves us cold?

Long before you get sexually excited by a particular individual, it seems you develop what's called a "love map." Deeply imbedded in your brain's circuitry, this map determines what arouses you sexually, and why you fall in love or lust with one person instead of another. People often seem to have a preference for faces similar to those that surrounded them as they grew up. In any event, through chance meetings and different experiences you layer additional imagery onto this map, and eventually a picture of "the perfect lover" emerges.

When you come across someone who fits your basic parameters, when the timing and mood and smells are right and touched with a bit of mystery, you fall in love. Though your love object may deviate in some respects from that perfect image in your head, you brush aside such concerns—for the moment.

Of course, there's not just one person out there for you. There are many who not only meet both your general and specific love criteria but might even love you back—all of which has great bearing not only on your marriage, but on your affairs as well.

What do people look for in long-term partners? The most desirable people are attractive with proportionate bodies. In other words, looks count, which is why people spend big dollars to improve theirs. Beauty—or the lack of it—is a screening device, a shorthand that lets us decide right away whether certain people are worth pursuing. There's even evidence that we pick potential lovers who share with us a similar level of attractiveness. And appearance is important for genetic reasons, not just aesthetic ones.

Starting from childhood, good-looking people tend to be more popular socially. They develop better interpersonal skills and so improve their chances at having better careers than their more homely brethren because of the jump-start their looks gave them. And, of course, women tend to cluster around good-looking men and vice versa.

> **FUN ADULTERY FACT**
>
> *Men get the best women
> they can afford, and women
> get the best men their
> looks can attract.*

Good-looking people have many more potential reproductive partners to choose from; they don't need to compromise as much, or go with the lesser evil. And when attractive people mate, either within or outside marriage, chances are that their children will be attractive too, and the cycle will perpetuate itself into the next generation. Researchers have even offered what's called the "sexy son" theory, which speculates that good-looking men who successfully attract good-looking women will create sons with the same knack, and on and on.

But even good-looking people have flaws and problems. Shyness, overt stupidity, infertility, bad character, bad taste, or addictions can easily negate the potential genetic bonanza that good looks promise at first glance. And we've all seen monumentally ugly people walking around with boy toys or trophy wives whom they wouldn't have had a chance in hell of attracting if looks were the sole criteria used in attracting a mate.

Still and all, whatever our own physical appeal (or lack thereof), most of us would rather sleep with an attractive person than an ugly one. And to the surprise of utterly no one, men choose women primarily on the basis of looks, youth, and health, traits that imply fertility.

Women, on the other hand, are a lot more interested in money and resources (just ask an average guy with average looks and an average car). But as we've seen, nature has its reasons. Women have far fewer shots at genetic immortality, and every kid counts. An inferior partner can burden her for a lifetime with inferior children. Therefore her mate must have not only the best genes she can attract, but also money and the potential to make more, the better to provide each child with every chance for success.

And—men, please take note—the competition for guys who can actually provide all this good stuff is fierce.

That's why they're often willing to do whatever it takes to land a guy—even become a mistress in the hopes of eventually becoming a wife or a mother.

So how do love maps work

> **FUN ADULTERY FACT**
>
> *There are no suitable, marriageable men available for millions of American women.*

in practice? Let's say, for example, that you're a guy, and your love map predisposes you toward tall brunettes with lively personalities. Just how many women in your city alone fit that general description? A hundred, a thousand? Granted you're not going to meet them all, but chances are you'll meet at least a few on your daily rounds to work, the gym, and the sports bar.

So why choose one tall brunette over another?

You'll bond with that one person because of specific personality traits that jibe with your desired characteristics, as well as timing, availability, proximity, smell (very important!), overall appearance, and, of course, a reciprocal interest in you. The more the total picture matches your internal love map, the more your body will pressure you, through intense infatuation, to mate with that particular person. And if that certain person wants to mate with you . . .

Well, by now we know the drill. PEA saturates the brain and your love object with its tantalizing possibilities and consumes your every waking moment. If those intense feelings persist, you might marry, in the process pledging to this person a lifetime of sexual and emotional fidelity just as society dictates you should. In a more perfect world, this all-consuming love would live as long as you do, and beyond.

So you settle in, buy a house, maybe have a child. Sure there are plenty of other lively brown-haired vixens out there but you're content—for the moment.

You stay in that chemical haze for a few years, long enough perhaps to see a baby through infancy, maybe even long enough to ensure it has a good chance for survival. But by now your overwhelming enthusiasm for Brunette #1 has faded; you've entered the disillusion zone. All those personality quirks that you pushed aside while courting start to grate. You're bored and restless.

And then, just by chance, you come across Brunette #2, who's not only the basic type that you like, but who also has even more compelling traits and characteristics—a person who adheres to your ever-evolving love map even more closely than your spouse does. And maybe you meet her under exciting or adventurous circumstances— on a camping trip or during an event fraught with drama and emotion. Personal interaction during an exciting event facilitates bonding in a big way.

The upshot? Well, if there's no real compatibility between you and your original brunette, and if you have only a superficial emotional bond and sense of shared responsibility, you're going to get antsy—kids, mortgages, or not. And once Brunette #2 appears, you might just stray, either casually or desperately, despite marital commitments and "prior claim" (the battle cry of the "wronged" spouse).

After all, as your body sees it, sex with Brunette #2 could well result in smarter, better-looking, and more successful children than the ones you've had with your spouse. It might result in better recreational sex and more fun than you've had in ages. And if the infatuation bug bites, there you are, back in romantic love again, only this time illicitly and with a lot more to lose.

On the other hand, both prior claim and your commitments to other people—especially existing children—really do matter. If the affair is discovered and you're forced into a divorce without really wanting one, your present comfort and genetic future might well be jeopardized. A bad lawyer or an onerous settlement can result in a lot less fun for you, just as abusive stepparents or a reduced standard of living can result in far less healthy and successful children.

And keep in mind that your infatuation with Brunette #2 will probably wear off too, only faster this time, since your body knows the score. So giving up half your worldly goods to marry her might not be smart. After all, the same pattern of infatuation/attachment/disillusion/dissolution is at work here, but often at an accelerated rate. Eventually you may want to leave #2 as well. For any number of reasons, your new brunette might be a better tactical, or short-term, than long-term choice. In other words, you may be better off maintaining a socially monogamous relationship with Brunette #1, and keeping your relationship with Brunette #2 at a strictly recreational level sex-wise.

But . . . but. Maybe Brunette #2 is the person you have been waiting for all these years. Maybe the children you create will be awesome, and your enhanced compatibility will result in happier childhoods for them too. Maybe "mature love" will be easier to find with this new person. Maybe you'll actually conceive with this new someone despite years of apparent infertility. The possibilities are endless and tantalizing.

So if you settle too quickly into a rut with Brunette #1, who might actually prove in the long run to be a poor choice, you could easily miss the chance for a more compatible match, and a happier life and offspring, down the road.

But if no other brunette fitting that description ever happens along, you could miss out on marriage and kids all together. Maybe no one else will ever want you. The penalties for choosing wrong in the love game are high, and don't forget it.

An ugly scenario, isn't it? Here you are, married to someone who at one time was the closest thing to perfection you thought you'd ever find. Then one day, you're at work or playing softball or sitting in a bar and someone else comes into your life who might easily be better suited in every way to the person you are *now*, not the one who settled for the first reasonably warm body that came along and was not nauseated at the sight of you.

Yet because you're married, society is telling you to deprive yourself of maybe true love or at least some ongoing recreational sex based on a commitment you made years ago in a chemical haze. And the penalties for disobeying society's dictates—as we will remind you over and over—can be brutal. How to know what's best?

Here is the true test of your body's (and mind's) ability to play nature's game. Though the chemistry can be very real when you meet a likely new prospect, and the feelings you have as a result of those reactions are beyond your conscious ability to control, your *reactions* to those feelings and the actions you take as a *result* of them are not.

Just because your body craves sex with someone new doesn't mean it's a great idea to be pursued full tilt.

It's the job of your higher self to consciously impose order and direction, based on the goals, commitments, beliefs, and ideals you've developed over time. Those beliefs and ideals may very well lead you to maintain sexual fidelity with Brunette #1, despite the baying hounds of temptation.

Or, you may decide to divorce and then mate with the new object of your affection, maybe leaving your current children to be raised by others, or taking them along with you, creating dislocation to which they may or may not be able to adapt.

Or, you may choose to stay in that marriage so rife with commitments—one boring but somewhat comforting in its stability—while still exploring your reproductive and emotional options on the side.

In other words, you may be ready for an affair.

PART II

THE ABC'S* OF ADULTERY

*(Always Be Cautious)

As a bartender served an attractive woman a glass of orange juice, the man sitting next to her said, "This is a special day; I'm celebrating."

"Me, too," she replied, clinking glasses with him.

"What are you celebrating?" he asks.

"Well, I've been trying to have a child for years, and today I found out I'm pregnant!"

"Congratulations," the man said. "As it happens, I'm a chicken farmer, and for years all my hens were infertile. But today they're finally fertile."

"How did it happen?"

"I switched cocks."

"What a coincidence," she said, smiling. "So did I."

CHAPTER 6

AFFAIR BASICS

*N*ow that we know why we want to cheat, let's start with the how's.

The potential for any given affair to destroy a marriage is usually estimated in terms of its length or intensity, but these can combine in odd ways. A one-night (or one-hour) stand can be a passionate, life-changing experience for someone in a loveless marriage. On the other hand, there are affairs based entirely on recreational sex that last for years.

As a general rule, the closer a lover's adherence to your love map and the more intense the infatuation and attachment, the longer the affair will last. The longer the affair, the more problematic it is for your marriage.

Whether they last an hour or a decade, affairs run on pretty much the same timetable as marriage, condensed to fit their often awkward circumstances:

 ◆ **INFATUATION**—you're attracted to each other.

- ◆ **ATTACHMENT**—you stay together long enough to at least have sex.

- ◆ **DISILLUSION**—second thoughts, guilt, neutrality, boredom set in.

- ◆ **DISSOLUTION**—you end the relationship, either voluntarily or not.

That's why it's often not worth chucking a serviceable marriage to marry an affair partner, since the relationship will probably run its course even faster than the marriage did. And, of course, you can get found out at any stage of this life cycle, rendering whatever plans you may have had moot, and your life a living hell. But more on that later.

There are three basic affair types:

- ◆ **ONE-NIGHT STANDS** (very short term)
- ◆ **SPORADIC AFFAIRS** (under six months)
- ◆ **SHADOW MARRIAGES** (over six months)

One-Night Stands

A one-night stand is a simple, spontaneous gene exchange. Your body perceives that casual sex with this particular person might serve a deeply buried reproductive need, so attraction kicks in and the rest of you follows suit. Often the parties involved know nothing but each other's names, and sometimes not even that. It's all about sex, pure and simple—wham bam thank you ma'am.

Assuming no STDs, vindictiveness, or other unpleasant surprises, these affairs are virtually never discovered unless you, for some silly reason, admit to them. Because again, while reproduction is the ultimate underlying goal of sex, most sane people have utterly no interest in actually producing a baby during trysts of these sorts. They are looking for relational or recreational sex, period.

Sporadic Affairs

Sporadic affairs last less than six months. You're on vacation or a business trip, you see someone, you mate numerous times. It's fun, exciting. You enjoy the novelty and share a few minor confidences but eventually return to the fold better for the experience.

Your body may perceive all this as a genuine reproductive alternative to your current relationship and induce you to see the lover a few more times. But often these affairs can be more trouble than they're worth. If they are, the infatuation and attachment highs will fade fast, and your interest will end.

This is the most common type of affair—clean, intense, but relatively uncomplicated. A little romantic hedonism over a few weeks or months, and then you move on. Act judiciously: choose your lover wisely, give only minimal details about your personal life, practice safe sex, and keep spouse and lover far apart, and the impact on your long-term relationship should be nil.

Yet sometimes even one-night stands turn into something more. Remember, you were attracted to this new person to begin with because of his or her adherence to your love map. Obviously there was something there that appealed to you, and sometimes that appeal can be overwhelming in the same way your spouse knocked you out at first.

And if the sex is really, really good—some researchers have even speculated that great sex may be an indicator of high genetic compatibility—maybe this is the person you've been practicing for all your life. Maybe this is your true love. Maybe . . . you've got to know.

Shadow Marriages

If the reproductive and emotional pull is that strong, a long-term affair or "shadow marriage" can easily evolve. A shadow marriage lets you mimic the benefits of serial monogamy without sacrificing the primary socially monogamous relationship on which you may be financially or emotionally dependent. By superimposing this shadow relationship on top of your legal one, you can go through the motions of serial monogamy without formal sanction or financial commitments.

A shadow marriage to a particular lover comes about when infatuation simply refuses to relinquish its hold. Yes, some long-term affairs are purely recreational, but many are based on closely shared love maps and compatibility, just like your marriage was. You feel much the same way about this new lover as you once did about your spouse. Maybe you'd even substitute this lover for your spouse, given a chance.

Unlike one-night stands and sporadic affairs, shadow marriages actually compete with more formal relationships. After all, here's a person who may be even better suited to the person you are now. Between you, you create your own rhythms, rituals, and amusements. Unconsciously seeing each other as good mating material, lovers build up some of the emotional ties that might have been necessary to see a child through infancy.

People sometimes go goofy during the infatuation stage of a shadow marriage. Their forbidden nature, combined with chemical highs, physical desires, and the emotional relief at maybe having found a "soul mate" and friend for life can lead people to do some pretty stupid things—like pledge eternal fealty to their lovers, or talk about divorce when, during rational moments, they intend no such thing.

But ultimately, the need for secrecy and the tacit understanding that this "marriage" will be temporary usually prevents you from making a full-scale commitment. A shadow marriage usually

FUN ADULTERY FACT

Only 5 percent of lovers in an affair end up marrying each other.

lasts, on average, between eighteen and twenty-nine months, going through its life cycle relatively quickly, a ghostly image of the more formal union.

As passionate and rewarding as affairs can be, they run out of steam the vast majority of the time. That's why it's generally not worth it to leave a functioning formal marriage just to embark on another, more tenuous relationship. An affair will probably run its course in short order anyway, leaving you with the desire to trade up once again, possibly at considerable financial and psychic cost.

And the reality is that illicit lovers rarely end up marrying each other anyway. Once divorced, people generally want to seek out someone new, who's unfettered by memories of the past, a past that the lover may have been too much a part of.

No matter what the length or intensity of an affair, the ties binding lover to lover are fragile indeed. Desire prompted by unconscious yearnings and yes, love, may keep you coming back to each other, but chances are these feelings will fade too, just as they did in your marriage.

After all, when you're together with a lover, you're both on your best behavior. You're not under the stress of all that day-to-day, petty, aggravating stuff that may have helped kill your affection for your spouse in the first place. If you're observing the 50-Mile Rule (remember—lover and spouse shouldn't live within fifty miles of each other), you may not even see your lover that often. There simply isn't the time, the space, or the freedom of movement so necessary for growing a deeper relationship.

So lovers rarely end up marrying each other, and when they do, the results are usually poor. There's something about changing an illicit lover to a spouse that changes things, generally for the worse.

But don't kid yourself. The end of any affair can be as wrenching and awful (for your lover, if not for you) as that of any formal marriage. No matter what the imperatives driving you to the relationship, once emotions are engaged, pain is almost sure to follow. Like marriages, affairs have life cycles, but also like marriage, individuals don't go through the stages at the same time.

Ultimately it's the weight of financial, child, and family responsibilities and a promise made long ago to have and to hold that keeps so many marriages together, sometimes past their expiration dates. Love affairs have no such ballast. Once the chemical attraction is gone, you move on, because you can.

CHAPTER 7

GETTING STARTED

*L*et's assume you're married with a child or two. Life is OK but dull, with no improvement in sight. For whatever reason, divorce isn't an option, but you wish it were. And while you're not consciously seeking an affair, you might not turn one down either, if the right person happened by.

Before he or she does, plan a little. Know what you want out of an extramarital relationship, should the opportunity arise.

Know Your Goals

Is recreational sex your primary interest and, if so, will occasional sex with different people do, or would a single long-term partner be more convenient, so you don't need to look for new candidates constantly? Do you want emotional or relational support too? Are you looking for kids, for fun, a way to get back at your spouse, or for new long-term marital or reproductive prospects? Know your goals!

Granted, your goals could change in a flash. An affair can start out as a simple gene exchange and surprise you by morphing into a full-blown shadow marriage lasting for years. Human relationships are dynamic, their outcomes impossible to predict. Affairs can be the most unpredictable relationships of all. You must never forget that once in an affair, you're basically a partner with someone who has the potential to screw you in ways you can't even imagine.

Choose Your Partners Wisely

If you're inclined to seek out a lover, as opposed to waiting for one to happen by, the Internet in particular has opened up a brave new world of possibility for adulterers, what with matchmaking sites, married-but-looking sites, swinger sites, and chat rooms of every description. While you absolutely can come across any number of weirdos and loons typing up a storm at three o'clock in the morning claiming to be six feet tall and Gable-esque, there are plenty of nice people mixed in with the freaks who are looking for someone just like you. (Just be careful to make the distinction.)

In fact, the need for discretion and a safe environment for adultery has led a German entrepreneur to set up a matchmaking service for marrieds looking to hook up with other marrieds. (One imagines that this brilliant idea will find its way to the United States soon.)

Plan Ahead

In any event, a little forethought will go a long way when that great new prospect who matches your love map comes along. If he or she is single, wants marriage and kids and says so, should you do him or her anyway, or do you bolt and look for a safer bet?

There's more to suitability than just adherence to a love map. A prospective lover must be available, interested, and discreet. She or he should want you more than need you and take pleasure in being with you, but have her or his own life beyond the relationship. She or he should accept your marital status as a given and know that the chances of marrying you are nil.

Always remember that you're entering potentially dangerous territory here. You *must* consider the implications of your actions before taking them. Don't just assume that things will turn out OK in the end. In other words . . .

Get Involved Slowly

Think before you act, and before you ask. A successful affair is one that enhances your real life without disturbing it. Or to put it another way, a successful affair is an undiscovered affair. There's no way to ensure this outcome, but the quickest way to ensure the opposite is to pick your partners indiscriminately and too close to home.

Never Play in Your Own Backyard . . . Unless You Want to Get Caught

Spouses and lovers should never live within fifty miles of each other. Preferably they should live in two different states. Their paths should never cross socially or professionally, for any reason at any time.

To sleep with people at your office or club or within your social circle is stupid beyond belief. Granted, hometown affairs have many seeming advantages such as convenience, proximity, and sometimes shared experiences—not to mention the chance to get to know a person a little before you go propositioning him or her.

But local relationships are virtually impossible to keep secret over time. Body language or chance sightings can give you away. Screwing around at work can destroy your career—and do you really want to deal on a daily basis with the marketing exec you dumped? Affairs with people like your husband's or wife's best friend are too absurd to even contemplate.

Out-of-town conventions, sporting events, and business trips provide some of the "safer" opportunities for seeking out affair partners, though it's best to avoid people who work in the same field you do, or who have any kind of connection to your business, such as a vendor.

Listen before You Leap

Let's say you love football. You live in Arizona, but you're on a business trip to Ohio and decide to visit the Football Hall of Fame for the weekend. While playing virtual quarterback for the Denver Broncos, you catch the eye of a woman far too good looking to actually be living in Canton. You're into blondes and she's just that, with a body that won't quit and a passing resemblance to your wife—seven years, two kids, and one mommy cut ago. She likes how you scramble in the pocket and you like her backfield.

Well, that's great, but before jumping into bed with your potential inamorata, before saying you're married, wine and dine her a bit. Learn a little about what makes her tick, what kind of relationships she's had, her long-term goals and desires.

Notice, please, how different this is from a first date when you weren't married, and when all you heard was blah, blah, blah while she talked about her job and her stupid roommate and what a drag her ex-boyfriend was. Your main concern then didn't extend much past booty call, so actually paying attention wasn't mandatory.

It is now. The risks are far higher, so listen up and pay attention. Difficult as it may be to resist, keep your zipper closed or your buttons buttoned and your ears open. Don't discuss your family, neighborhood, or employer. Don't hand out a business card.

Be cautious in what you share. Remember—any information

you offer can end up grist for the mill of someone who wants to get back at you for reasons real or imagined. (Hell, it could be a ringer hired by your wife to see whether or not you *will* cheat. Why give her the satisfaction?)

By listening carefully you may discover that she's totally wrong for you, her football obsession notwithstanding. If so, say good night. You've lost a few bucks but nothing else, and your marital status has remained a nonissue. But if you decide to move ahead . . .

Take Only Pleasure, and Leave Behind Nothing Incriminating

If you end up in bed (lucky devil), go to your new lover's hotel room, not yours. And don't leave too much personal stuff around. More than one one-night stand has rifled his or her lover's pockets for cash, credit, and business cards.

And forget about falling asleep in some postcoital glow—no cuddling! Leave when you're done. There may be a good flick on HBO you don't want to miss. Don't linger.

Be Up Front about Your Marital Status if You Want to See Him or Her Again

Lay out the ground rules first. There's no good time to say "I'm married," which is why people often "forget," but it's generally best to have this pesky detail out front once you've decided to go start a relationship.

Everyone is capable of flying a false flag when it comes to sex, men in particular, but if you end up in a longer-term affair or shadow marriage, don't continue to pose as single, separated, or divorced if it isn't true.

Why? Well, your new lover may already be dreaming about a life with you, dreams you're probably doing nothing to discourage because either you don't realize what your lover's up to or because you're in your own chemical haze. When the fog parts, however, and your lover realizes that you've been taking her for a ride literally and figuratively—in other words, when she somehow ferrets out that you're married and have been leading her on—"revenge" may be too mild a word for what comes next.

Of course, since at any given time it's generally true that "all the good ones are taken," any sexually active adult beyond age twenty-five would pretty much have to be an idiot not to realize how slim the chances are of finding someone really cool who's not already married. (On the other hand, hope does spring eternal.)

As the married partner in this little scenario, you don't necessarily need to feel sorry for the person who's been led down the garden path—just be aware that their perception of what constitutes "available" may have nothing to do with yours. If you don't lay the proper groundwork (so to speak), you'll be unpleasantly surprised by the fall-out. It's better to let your extracurricular squeeze know that she or he is running in permanent second position, and let them decide to deal with you or not.

Don't Just Assume That Your Marital Status Is a Negative

A relationship with you could be satisfying important needs for your affair partner—your marital status isn't necessarily a negative. If your lover tells you to get lost, well, you haven't revealed too much after all. If he or she wants to think about it, call in a few days (never from home, office, or cell phone—plenty of people have caller ID, and use it).

And follow your instincts. While another rendezvous may help you determine whether or not this person is worthy of serious pursuit, it could also be an opportunity for someone you've angered with your admission of marriage to seek some quick and easy revenge.

Don't Get Greedy

There's always a tendency when you first start a new relationship to wallow in it and take every ounce of pleasure as quickly as you can. Understandable, but never a good idea. As we'll see, compartmentalization—keeping the worlds occupied by your spouse and your lover completely separate—is a vital part of affair management. Sure you want to suck up every ounce of happiness that life has suddenly put on offer, but greed is the quick path to disclosure, accidental or otherwise.

Much like the first time you saw your spouse, you may become a blithering basketcase, but this time over someone utterly inappropriate that you meet by chance. There's nothing like lust to energize a stagnant existence, which is precisely why rationality must prevail.

Though a tempestuous outside liaison might be a lot more satisfying than your marriage is at this point, before getting involved with *any* lover beyond a one-night stand, ask yourself:

◆ Is this person willing to abide by my terms?

◆ How do I organize our meetings?

◆ How do I get out of this once things run their course?

◆ What happens if my spouse finds out?

◆ What are my postmarriage contingency plans?

Until you have answers that you can live with, don't move ahead.

No matter how careful you are, things can—and often will–go wrong. People lie about having STDs. An awesome lay may end up shaking you down for abortion money, then

> **NOT SO FUN ADULTERY FACT**
>
> *Even one-night stands can be risky business.*

thoughtfully send a picture of the baby she decided to keep to your wife. Hell, think of *Fatal Attraction*! These things do happen.

Even with rigorous adherence to the rules laid down, there is no guarantee that something won't go wrong—there are simply too many variables when it comes to human nature. There's always risk involved, even that of falling in love with a person you can't marry.

So why get involved in an affair to begin with, given the risks?

Affairs Can Be the Saving Grace of Marriage

A well-managed affair can be a wondrous mixture of great sex, affection, emotional support, and joy. Lovers can be a revelation. They like you for the person you've become, not for the person you were. They even laugh at your jokes, and when was the last time your spouse did that?

Lovers appreciate exactly the aspects of your personality that your spouse has come to ignore or even despise. The secret fantasy life you create outside of marriage—we call it Affair World—is one where commitments and responsibilities are to another person alone, not to property and propriety and the forces of convention.

Just where is Affair World? It's that secret place that you occupy with your current lover. Whether you fashion it in a hotel room, at a resort, or at a "bachelor" pad (never, ever the house you occupy with your spouse!), it's the place to test out the new, enhanced "you" who has evolved and changed over the years, the new person whom your spouse would either not recognize or would hold in contempt because he or she knows you too well (or thinks so, anyway).

Affair World is a place to stretch and experiment, a place for new experiences and rekindled emotions. There's irony here. One of the great things about having an affair is the seeming ability to let your hair down. Here's a willing, sometimes adoring person who's not only accepting of who you are right now, but who wants you too! No preconceived notions, no emotional baggage, but a fresh start, a chance to take what you've learned over the last few years and apply it without fear of ridicule. You'll want to wallow in these great new sensations and keep them close by 24/7.

Don't.

Show too much relief, too much pleasure, too much of anything at home, and you're sure to give the game away. It's easy to forget when you're caught up in great sex and a glimpse of the world as you'd like it to be that things at home need to stay pretty much the same in order to maintain domestic tranquillity.

Successful affairs come about through a combination of good instincts, good taste in partners, good behavior, and good luck, all leavened with a large dollop of common sense. The smart Big Head never lets lust lead the charge toward infidelity.

CHAPTER 8

MANAGING THE HOME FRONT

Whatever your marriage happens to be at the start of an affair is what it had better remain. Wholesale or even subtle changes in looks, attitudes, or habits can be a sure tip-off that something new is going on in your life, so your behavior had better remain consistent with history and expectation.

Introduce New Behaviors with Care

Sure, people change even if they aren't catting around on the side. A friend has a heart attack and you change your eating habits. You read an article about online trading and decide to give up your broker of ten years. It happens.

But if your real motive in learning tennis, for example, is to keep up with your new squeeze, don't just run out for lessons if you've been a couch potato for the last five years. And don't sneak lessons on the sly either—you'll have a hell of a time explaining why you didn't "share" this information with your spouse.

Instead, find a convincing subtext for this new interest, one that the spouse and kids can share. (Watching the tennis pro running around in shorts is *not* a good reason, by the way.) Maybe you can all stand to lose some weight. Maybe the club would be a good place for the kids to make new friends.

However you go about it, be careful how you indulge your new fitness habit outside the family orbit. If you live in the Midwest for example, and it's colder than the balls on a brass monkey, it probably won't do to come back tan from a tennis rendezvous in Arizona when you're supposed to be in Omaha.

Also, certain types of sporting equipment leave tell-tale marks— blisters from golf clubs, those funny checks on your hands from cycling gloves. Injuries happen too. (Just imagine the phone call to your spouse from an emergency room in Vail when your itinerary said L.A. . . . 'nuff said.)

Just as your spouse's habits are ingrained (which is what makes this person boring and predictable in the first place), so should yours be when you're home. Even if your lover introduces you to a brave new world of culture, movies, sexual positions, whatever, the place to indulge in these things is with your lover, not with your spouse.

Keep Your Tastes the Same

If you've always listened to classic rock for example, don't suddenly make a public shift to obscure jazz or Howard Stern. Don't mention the movie you saw with your lover when you haven't been to a theater with your spouse in two years.

And no, now is not the time for the hair transplant or breast implants, to update your wardrobe or your lingerie drawer, or to start wearing briefs when you've worn boxers forever.

Keep Your Sex Life the Same

Don't go changing routines here unless your spouse wants it, in which case you should be wondering what *he or she* is up to. Don't vary the frequency or the positions or the amount of consideration you show without being prompted to do so. And don't insist on new techniques that your lover adores but your mate finds abhorrent.

Don't Lie about Your Whereabouts

Even if your lover goes with you on a business trip or vacation, be where you say you're going to be, whether it's the Hilton in Columbus or a motorcycle race in Fresno.

Sure there's a risk that your spouse or some friend might spontaneously decide to drop in. But chances are, if you're out of town a few states away (observing as always the 50-Mile Rule) and in regular contact with home, you'll be in the clear. The last thing you need is for your spouse to call the hotel with a real emergency, only to find that you're not even checked in.

Cell phones are a blessing for those of us who'd just as soon not part with our itineraries, but be careful with them. Consistently refusing to give out a hotel or emergency number in addition to your mobile number can be a red flag too.

Don't Change Your Spending Habits

A string of one-night stands, not to mention a full-blown affair, can be expensive. There's alcohol, food, hotels, travel—even with expense accounts these things add up. Just don't let them add up on your personal credit card bills, and don't let them eat into monies you should be spending to maintain your home and family. Remember, women in particular seek resources. Any change in that resource level back at the ranch will be duly noted. By the same token, don't start suddenly buying gifts for your spouse or kids if you aren't habitually generous. This is a sure sign that you've got something to hide.

Keep Your Home Inviolate

How many times have you watched a TV show where the harried adulterer ends up in her home office, whispering "I told you never to call me here" to the dope on the other end of line? Stupid, right? Yet married lovers find themselves in such predicaments constantly. Monitoring phone messages, sorting frantically through the mail, trying to explain why e-mail passwords should remain secret—nothing could be more pathetic, or obvious, than these lame attempts to carve out a little privacy for yourself.

In the old days, intercepted phone calls, private investigators, letters, and receipts were by far the most common ways that affairs were revealed. Nowadays e-mail, cell phone bills, wireless text messages, photo-cams, and seducers-for-hire have joined the party. In any event, when it comes to preserving the sanctity of your home, you can't pick a lover too carefully. "Never contact me at home" should be the first ground rule you lay down. Ideally your lover shouldn't even know where you live. A sign of distrust? No, of prudence.

Figure it this way. With your name and social security number—and often just your name and a city—a lover can track

> ### DEPRESSING ADULTERY FACT
>
> *Your communications are not secure, whether at home, on the road, or in the office.*

you down on the Internet for less than fifty dollars. The answer to "who the hell is calling at this hour" can be revealed by caller ID or * 69 (how apropos). Your computer can inadvertently give you away via the "history" button, which tracks all the sites you've visited, and today there's a whole set of surveillance programs and "bots" that track and copy not only the text of your e-mails, but your travels through your favorite porn sites or wherever.

You should check in with your lover regularly so that he or she doesn't feel the need to contact you. If you can't remember the phone number, write it down without the area code. And as we said, be careful with pagers and cell phones. They only *seem* more private than your home phone, and somewhere some moron with a Radio Shack scanner may be monitoring your intimate conversations—and looking to cash in.

If you must hear from your inamorata during the week, give him or her your direct office number and create a playful "secret identity" so a real name is never revealed to a secretary or voice mail.

Your assistant can be recruited into your spouse's service, by the way—more than one affair has been derailed when a secretary balked at being a go-between for a boss and his or her lover. Don't count on loyalty when it comes to affairs. You're frankly better off with no middleman at all.

When you call your lover, use prepaid phone cards, not the telephone credit card that's billed to your house, and have a good excuse handy as to why you have one—better yet, keep it hidden. But if you've never walked the family dog in your life (shame on you), don't start just so you can use the pay phone down the street. It's a break in routine that *will* be noticed.

Children First

At heart, affairs may be about seeking a better reproductive legacy, but this doesn't give you the right to neglect existing children in pursuit of some "ideal child" who will probably never materialize. Every child you have a hand (or whatever) in creating is your responsibility, no matter who the other parent or the circumstance, period.

Never introduce your children to a lover. *Never* allow them to see you with a lover. *Never* talk to your kids about your other lives. *Never* use your kids as pawns against your spouse, no matter how much you may have come to loathe him or her. It's not the kids' fault. They deserve a childhood free of adult cares. Remember—your children are flying your genetic flag, so don't screw them up any more than you already have.

Don't Let Emotions Give You Away

During the infatuation stage of a sporadic affair or shadow marriage, you're going to be walking an emotional tightrope. All you want is to be with this new person—anything that keeps you away is an imposition. It sucks! (Or not, as the case may be.) Completely understandable, but it's exactly this kind of thing that makes compartmentalization so important.

If you've been pretty much dead to your marriage the last few years (and who hasn't?), sudden displays of affection are going to look pretty suspicious, as will emotional withdrawal if by nature you're affectionate. And please, avoid those little private smiles that come so easily when your lover comes to mind. They imply secret knowledge, and the zealot you live with (so consumed with creating "intimacy" with you) is going to want to know where your good mood came from.

Be Here Now

"Be here now" is a touchy-feely expression that applies perfectly to affairs. It means to be fully engaged in whatever world you are occupying at the moment, to the exclusion of all others. When you're home, adapt yourself completely to that environment, leaving the affair as an afterthought. When you're with your lover, put your energy there.

As we've seen, affairs provide tactical options within a long-term marriage strategy, but in the great scope of things they are probably not that important. Keeping your extramarital relationships secret and separate helps you maintain the illusion of free choice while letting your spouse maintain both dignity and a sense of stability. Keep the two worlds separate, with the neutral zone intact. As we'll see, compartmentalization is a key element to a successful affair—or marriage.

CHAPTER 9

MANAGING AFFAIR WORLD

*A*successful affair is one that enhances your life without disturbing it. In other words, a successful affair is one that remains secret. Of course, the horrors of discovery could all be in your head, but do you really want to test that theory?

Affair management means compartmentalizing and keeping control of both of the worlds in which you reside. You are, after all, playing to two audiences—lover and spouse. People and emotions aren't necessarily predictable, but marriage and affair life cycles are. Since you now know what to expect at each stage, you can anticipate potential issues and tailor your actions accordingly.

Affairs Are for Enjoyment, Not Added Stress

Though reproduction is in many ways the driving force behind sexual urges, actually *creating* a child outside of wedlock isn't precisely a rational or desirable goal for most people. So if an affair isn't fun, there's no point in having one, period.

No Emotional Divas, Please

The last thing you want is some titanic test of will pitting you against a disaffected lover—or worse, the lover and your spouse. Lovers aren't trophies to be displayed, but diversions to be enjoyed. Give an affair too high priority in your life—or pick someone who gives it too high priority in *theirs*—and a brief dalliance can destroy your peace of mind. A small detour off the matrimonial highway can turn into a fifty-car collision.

Yes, you might get involved with someone so absolutely right for you that the relationship becomes painful. Hearts do break; lovers can feel very strongly about each other indeed. That's what love is all about, after all.

The danger here is twofold: your own emotional involvement and that of the lover who wants you just as intensely or even more so, no matter what the cost. However cynical *you* might be about marriage, it can be a seductive goal indeed if your lover is single and hates it. But part of affair management is managing expectations. There simply cannot be any.

Yet if you find yourself in a position where a lover has truly changed your life, maybe divorce should become an option. Existence in general can be miserable enough without putting yourself through marital hell on a daily basis. It could be that your lover is truly the right person for you at this point in time. Why deprive yourself?

Choose Your Lovers Wisely

It should be obvious that picking the right affair partner is a vital part of a stress-free extramarital relationship. Even with the right partner, plenty of things can happen to blow your cover. Sometimes these can't be predicted—car accidents, medical emergencies—but carelessness and ego often can be.

While Affairs May Occupy Your Mind, They Rarely Occupy Your Time

Affair management isn't just a question of how best to deal with your lover, who might be taking up, what, 1 percent of your time? 5 percent maybe (not counting the time you spend daydreaming and mooning)?

It's just as critical not to give yourself away the other 95 percent of the time while you're at home. That way you're free to pursue your outside interests without interference. Once engaged in an affair you're playing to two audiences: spouse and lover. Each has different expectations, needs, and opinions with regard to you. As we've already mentioned, any radical changes in lifestyle or attitude are sure to be noticed times two. This is in large part how covers get blown and lives wrecked.

Compartmentalization Is Key to Successful Affair Management

In *The Crack-Up,* F. Scott Fitzgerald wrote, "The test of a first-rate intelligence is the ability to hold two opposed ideas in the mind at the same time and still retain the ability to function." That's what makes for a first-class adulterer too!

Your marriage and affair must exist in two different worlds. What you get out of each relationship is different—if you're smart and lucky, never the twain shall meet. One is for practical day-to-day living, and the other is for passion, sex, and fun. When you hold these relationships completely separate, with a neutral zone in between, there's never a question of allegiance because you're completely aligned with the world you're living in at the moment. Learn to feel comfortable with two separate emotional identities and never let them overlap, literally or figuratively.

Silence Is Golden

"Loose lips sink ships," as the old saying goes—if you want to keep USS *Affair* skimming happily along the Extramarital Sea, maintain total silence about your activities, and insist that your

> **FUN ADULTERY FACT**
>
> About 5 percent of married men and women cheat in any given year.

lover do the same. Don't tell friends, relatives, coworkers, children, or anyone else. Don't flaunt the hot chick who's wild for you in front of your business associates. After all, what people don't know, they can't talk about, right?

Don't Take Affairs Personally

Remember, there are hundreds, if not thousands of people out there who meet your love map criteria and vice versa. Don't buy into what your body and emotions might be saying about any specific new lover. Chances are that person won't be the love of your life any more than your spouse is.

It's easy enough to say "don't take this seriously," but it is something else to actually create distance from the emotions a lover can stir in you. Every person in a relationship starts out as a type. Single guys usually get this without questioning it—all they want is a quick bang and onto the next. Only in time can you come to see a lover as a full-fledged individual, and time is one of the things that most affairs, even shadow marriages, lack.

Keep Your Affairs Distant

Here we are, back at the 50-Mile Rule. Remember—your separate worlds will be that much easier to maintain if there's no social or geographic overlap. There's no telling how many marriages have come to an ugly, unnecessary end because the affairs that made them bearable were conducted too close to home.

So it should go without saying—I hope—that your lover will never set foot in your house (or city or state for that matter). The two of you will never make love in the bed you share with your spouse. No used condoms will ever just "appear" in the trashcan. No one will ever cut your wife's face out of your wedding pictures or put a link on your computer that shows the two of you naked in bed. No one will check through the prescription cabinet or leave an earring or cufflink on the vanity.

And speaking of condoms—use them, but remember that DNA testing is getting cheaper all the time, so dispose of them carefully and thoroughly. More than one high-profile athlete has gotten nailed by a groupie who followed up a quickie with a turkey baster and voilà, ended up nine months later with a bouncing little annuity all her own. There's an outfit in Europe that sells a "do-it-yourself" sperm detection test—just the thing to help determine what you may have been up to in the back seat of the new car. And speaking of cars . . .

Safe Sex Means Safe Locations Too

"Safety" is, of course, a relative concept when it comes to places for sex—among the best bets is your lover's place (if he or she is single, of course). But no matter how convenient, don't leave clothes or easily identifiable items behind, items that could find their way back to your house in a box addressed to your spouse once you've kicked the latest lover to the curb.

The hotel you've checked into on business is another logical place for sex—one with on-demand porn and room service no less! But be careful in your dealings with the staff. Customer service is a big thing these days, and you don't want the concierge greeting the spouse-who-looks-like-your-lover (remember your love map) at the hotel when your spouse has never been there before in his or her life.

Cars make lousy trysting sites. They are notorious clue collectors—matchbooks, business cards, jewelry, press-on nails, odd stains on the upholstery . . . yuck! And anyway, car sex was more fun when cars were bigger and you were thinner. Avoid it.

Don't Expect Any Affair to Last

Everyone wants love everlasting, or at least we think we do. But remember, fading chemical attraction is actually a protective mechanism, a way to keep your options open by cutting the emotional bonds holding you to one particular spouse or lover.

Don't impart any kind of mystical, transcendent, once-in-a-life-time significance to any given affair. Chances are that this too will pass, just as the excitement in your marriage did, only to reappear when you meet someone new. Consider it nature's thumb in the eye, just for you.

The problem is that everyone has a different timetable when it comes to falling out of love. Some people never do. But getting a lover to relinquish you when the time comes is a vital part of managing Affair World.

Create No Expectations

That's why you must be prudent in word and deed with your lover. For the most part, the joy and sexual fulfillment you feel in an extramarital relationship are fleeting at best. Never give your lover cause to think otherwise.

Realize That Power Will Shift as the Affair Progresses

It's often easier when both partners in an affair are married, since they know from the get-go the limitations imposed by their respective relationships. The power to set the agenda shifts depending on timing and each person's circumstance.

In a married/single relationship, it's the married partner who sets the agenda during the infatuation, attachment, and disillusion stage. A single woman in particular will often adhere to just about any agenda you set—until you decide to call it quits. Then you may well be at her mercy.

Why? Here's a woman who may be leading a boring, unhappy life with few dates and little sex. If she's in her twenties, she may have some bargaining power based on youth or looks, but if she's older, her options may be looking dim. All of a sudden she's a mistress, embroiled in what she may well consider a dramatic, passionate relationship with great implications for her future. Every dinner-and-sex tryst becomes a major event. She'll do anything to keep the good stuff coming.

A single woman in an affair is hoping against hope, trying to buck the odds. And given those odds, it's no surprise that her main aim in life could easily be wresting you from your spouse's grip.

So she'll remain subservient in the relationship as long as she senses hope of getting what she really wants, social and sexual legitimacy as a person in whom you'll make a long-term legally sanctioned investment.

It's during the dissolution stage of an affair—the most dangerous part naturally—that the single lover finally gets the upper hand. Suddenly she or he is in a position to control your destiny, based on sometimes extensive personal knowledge (if you've been stupid enough to share some). If your lover feels rejected or discarded, she or he may want to make your life as miserable as you've made hers or his.

Be Honest about the Future

Unless you set the no-divorce rule early and refrain from voicing idle daydreams about a possible future together, your lover is going to read whatever he or she wants into the relationship, and what your lover wants is you and all the good stuff he or she believes comes along with you.

Never talk to your lover about your spouse, your kids, your house, your dreams of sailing around the world, or anything pertaining to your life at home.

Honesty here means being truthful yet kind with regard to the lover who may get hurt in the relationship. It doesn't mean revealing your secret self. You should no more bare your soul to a lover than you would to your spouse.

Just as you shouldn't spin a long-term lie about your marital status, never lie about what good things the future may hold for you and your lover together if there aren't any. That's what honesty means in this context.

Be Careful about Gifts and Help

Excessive generosity to your lover will increase expectations while feeding secret despair that he or she can't latch onto someone as nice as you permanently. This can really backfire down the road.

It's a fine line. You're having an affair to have some fun, explore some different aspects of your personality, and maybe change your reproductive or social destiny. If your lover is truly a partner in this endeavor, he or she deserves appreciation and recognition—just not a gift more opulent and expensive than the one you gave your spouse for your tenth anniversary.

Remember—no matter how many times you say that the relationship has no real future, your lover may still find great significance in words and deeds that were, for you, just throwaways. These are the things that will come back to haunt you once your lover holds the whip hand.

Don't Rely on the Code of Silence

Yes, there *is* a code of silence regarding affairs. Most of your friends and associates will keep your secret (of course, it takes only one who won't). Men in particular are usually envious as hell when one of their buddies gets lucky. They'll keep their mouths shut in particular because they don't want to get their own wives all worked up about your infidelity. But don't count on the code to keep your secrets safe. A chance comment—or sighting—can still rock your world.

Remember That You're Always at Risk

No matter how carefully you try to go about your business, you *can get caught*. Exposure might come about from something as simple as being seen together by some friend of your spouse's who decided to play hooky one day. Or your husband might hire an investigator or tap your e-mail or cajole a drunken confession out of your best friend or hook up one of those "Truster" doo-dads on the phone without your knowledge.

Even well-managed affairs can be found out for stupid reasons unrelated to some mistake you made. Risk is a built-in part of infidelity. Make sure those risks are worth it, because there's one thing we can guarantee, with complete confidence—once caught your life will become a living hell. Do everything you can to avoid this fate.

Know When to Call It Quits

There comes a time in almost every affair, whether it lasts fifteen minutes or fifteen years, when disillusion sets in and the effort of keeping up the charade exceeds the benefits. Ending an affair is a lot harder than getting into one. But if you've been discreet, revealed little personal information, made few promises, and created no expectations, you'll be well ahead of the game when the time comes to pull the plug.

Remember—for many if not most people, affairs are recreation, just a more complicated form of booty call. If you want nothing out of it but to get in and get out, it's important to hook up with someone who's got similar goals in mind.

CHAPTER 10

ENDING AN AFFAIR

*L*ike marriages, affairs work best when both lovers are working toward mutually agreed upon ends. But again, like marriages, this is rarely the case.

The sad fact is that you and your lover will move through the affair life cycle at different speeds. Even at the infatuation stage, physiological and psychological factors will be working hard to pull you apart. Eventually they'll probably succeed, just as they succeeded in putting a damper on your marriage. Then what?

Well, if your spouse ever figures out what you're up to, the point may be moot. (Ever notice how the people most adamantly against adultery are usually those whom no one else would ever want to sleep with anyway?) But virtually every affair must end. A well-managed one has a much better chance of trickling to a civil halt. A poorly managed one is far more likely to blow up in your face. And there's nothing like having a rabid, scorned lover-turned-psycho on your case to really foul up your day.

WHY DO AFFAIRS END?

♦ One or both partners meet someone new.

♦ You're found out.

♦ The chemistry ends.

♦ The married lover gets a conscience (not recommended).

♦ The married lover fails to get a divorce.

♦ The married lover gets a divorce, but dumps the affair partner and finds someone else.

♦ One or the other affair partners turns vindictive.

Of course, sometimes an illicit relationship ends because the affair partners marry each other, but this happens so rarely it's barely worth noting.

Endings Are Rarely by Mutual Agreement

The decision to end an affair is almost always made unilaterally. Usually the person who started the relationship in the first place—generally the married partner—wants out first. Far from feeling remorse about leaving the relationship, you may feel like a burden has been lifted. The person you're dumping, of course, may feel far differently.

There's No Best Way to End an Affair

Just a lot of bad ones, each fraught with risk (but you knew that when you started down this path). At the very least, someone is going to end up with hurt feelings, if not a butt kicking. Rejection hurts. Loss of affection hurts. Losing all those free meals hurts. In any event, pain is often the only thing left to fill the void, and such pain can be substantial. It's this pain combined with anger and humiliation that can lead rejected lovers to lash back.

Once you want out, you want out fast. But some extraction methods are riskier than others:

THE "NIT-PICKING" APPROACH. The partner wanting out starts picking arguments about minor things like clothing or table manners or weight that meant nothing when the affair was going hot and heavy.

THE "CANCELING A TRIP WITHOUT CALLING" APPROACH. Always a popular favorite, though it has an undesirable side-effect—the person getting blown off is often reduced to calling around frantically to see if you're OK.

THE "DON'T-PUT-THAT-CALL-THROUGH" APPROACH. Making a lover suddenly persona non grata is a quick way to ensure that he or she will just fade away quietly—*not*.

THE "SPEAK TO MY LAWYER" APPROACH. Letting someone else do your dirty work for you.

In other words, ignore, embarrass, or inconvenience this now-extraneous person a few times and surely she or he will "get it," maybe without having to be told in so many words.

Well, maybe. On the other hand, your jilted lover might be inspired to get *you*. And no matter how careful you've been, if the affair has lasted any time at all, chances are there's plenty of ammunition, stockpiled and waiting.

Be Smart from the Start

Endings need not be traumatic. After all, with no expectations or illusions about the relationship as anything but a respite from real life, it can be a relatively simple matter—though not necessarily a painless one—to agree that parting is inevitable.

By the time it comes to this, your lover may sense that something's amiss anyway. Maybe you aren't calling much. Maybe the two of you haven't seen each other in three months when in the past it was every couple of weeks.

Gradually phasing things out can be a good strategy, since your lover can adjust his or her life accordingly, learning along the way that life is indeed possible without you. But "phasing out" isn't the same as "blowing off." Eventually your lover will want to know what's going on, and he or she deserves an answer.

But if you instead decide that you can't be bothered and tell your receptionist to stop taking calls or if you cancel your e-mail address or just quit responding to your lover's messages, you may easily create a potentially lethal enemy, one who might call you fifty times a night—at home—until you deign to get on the phone.

One Way Guaranteed to Backfire Big Time

Let's say you're scared of exactly what will happen when you *do* pull the plug. So instead of decreasing involvement, you increase it, hoping that this frenetic burst of energy will disguise your lack of interest while staving off your lover's demands that you get divorced—gaining you a little breathing room while you figure out how to extricate yourself.

What you've done is increased expectations a hundredfold. Think of it from your lover's perspective. Here's a person who's been in an affair for months, maybe years, and all of a sudden you're frantically recommitting yourself! Could it be anything but love, the real kind, the kind you divorce for?

Imagine your lover's reaction when you say, "It's over." "Enraged" is too mild a word.

Who Owes What to Whom?

Whatever the approach, you're betting that your soon-to-be-ex-lover's overwhelming affection and lingering respect for you are going to override a lust for vengeance. That's ego talking. Don't just assume a willingness on his or her part to keep the affair a lifetime secret just so that *you* can go merrily on your way, lavishing sex and attention on someone else.

But you will probably come off better by phasing things out gradually and bringing closure—in person—to the situation. A tactful, more thoughtful approach is more likely to yield the end results you're looking for: no further entanglement and no exposure.

> **NOT SO FUN ADULTERY FACT**
>
> *Former lovers have no real investment in keeping you happy . . . or keeping your secrets.*

How to Say That the Party's Over

When the time comes to formally end the relationship, do it kindly but without excuses. Your approach should be specifically tailored to your lover's personality. By this time, you ought to know what buttons *not* to push and how much "stuff" has been accumulated in terms of gifts, cards, and letters—all those things we've already warned you about.

If your reasons for ending the affair are cruel (and they inevitably are)—boredom, someone else, chemical burnout, whatever—cushion the blow. To call your lover and blithely say, "I've lost interest in this relationship, so I'm not going to call you anymore and don't call me. Good-bye" is both callous and cowardly. (Maybe you *do* deserve to get nailed at that.)

Instead, end it gently, in person if you can, although not in public. Tell your lover that he or she means a lot to you and always will, but that circumstances have changed and it's time to move on. The ending you both knew was coming has arrived. If your lover gets upset, be comforting, but don't give any reason to think you'll change your mind. Then leave!

An alternate approach is to say that you've decided to recommit to your partner. This has a nice, heroic ring to it even if it's BS, but this definitely won't work if you violate the 50-Mile Rule and have affairs within your social or work circle. A former lover needs only to look at your interaction (or lack thereof) with your spouse at an office get-together or party, or see you with someone new, to know that you were lying. Revenge will be both forthcoming and swift.

Before leaving your now ex-lover for what you hope will be the last time, offer to call in a couple of weeks just to see how he or she is doing, then keep your word. He or she may well be going through a grieving process. Make sure progress is being made toward exorcising you from his or her life.

A Few Words About Grief

It can take a year or more to go through the grieving process (a long time to realize that you're vulnerable to someone else's whims and moods). The process consists of:

- ◆ **DENIAL AND ISOLATION**
- ◆ **ANGER** (rage, envy, hatred, resentment)
- ◆ **BARGAINING** (promises, threats, compromises)
- ◆ **DEPRESSION** (loss and loneliness)
- ◆ **ACCEPTANCE** (understanding, giving up, moving on)

You probably skipped through the whole process in five minutes, so relieved were you to be done with the whole thing. The problem, of course, is that your former lover might get stuck in the anger/bargaining/depression stages.

If he or she threatens you with exposure at this point, try to reason with them, over the phone if you can, in person if you must. Sometimes calling their bluff—saying, "Go ahead, call my spouse if you want to"—is a way to defuse the situation, since it allows the ex-lover to blow off steam without actually acting on the threat. As a last resort, call an attorney about possible legal action. But frankly, you may well be screwed—it's bad juju when a person who can do great harm to your marriage is actually motivated to do so.

As we all know, jilted lovers can become incredibly vindictive and obsessive. While they may not contact your husband or wife directly, there are, of course, a million and one other ways to make a point, and a world of neighbors, kids, and coworkers to talk with. Stalking, paternity suits, forged letters, viral e-mails, private detectives, skywriting—the possibilities are endless.

Imagine a billboard near your office, where a man (not your husband) proclaims his love for you in letters ten feet high. Or those naked pictures you took of each other, digitized and posted on the Web. Or a videotape of your latest kinky romp, surreptitiously placed in your kid's VCR, just waiting for the moment he wants to see his favorite cartoon. People can be incredibly creative when it comes to righting what they perceive to be wrongs.

Having followed the course of action outlined in this book faithfully, you've limited your exposure to a possible onslaught. Nevertheless, despite your very best efforts, you may have chanced onto someone desperate and unreasonable. Hope for the best, but batten down the hatches. You may be in for the worst time of your life.

PART III

TRUTH & CONSEQUENCES

A married woman unexpectedly walks into the bedroom she shares with her husband to find him going at it with an attractive young thing. She sputters, stamps her feet, and hurls all sorts of invective, but only when she accuses him of adultery does he rise to his feet, stunned.

"An adulterer? Me? Never!"

"Yes, you!" she spits back. "The evidence is lying there naked in our bed!"

And indeed the young lovely is there plain as day, but the husband replies, brazen as you please, "Who are you going to believe—your own eyes or me?"

CHAPTER 11

Dignity & Denial

*A*s we all too often forget, actions have consequences. No matter how careful or discreet your infidelities, the risk of discovery *always* exists—and once found out, you're in deep doo-doo. It's as simple, and as complicated, as that.

The main reason for compartmentaliz- ing your life and keep- ing your affairs secret and out of the way is

NOT SO FUN ADULTERY FACT

There is no "good explanation"—at least one that your spouse will accept— for cheating.

that such discretion spares your spouse—and by extension, you—a lot of aggravation. Secrecy has nothing to do with mitigating the "guilt" you probably aren't feeling anyway. Guilt is a control mechanism transmitted from one generation to the next to secure your obedience to society's norms and customs.

Love of another person is rarely the issue in a triangle situation. You can feel great respect and mature love for your spouse while still seeking sex and stimulation on the side. Love alone won't prevent you from having an affair, but having an affair doesn't mean that your spouse isn't respected.

In fact, men often see their wives as paragons of virtue. Only she is strong enough to put up with him, to cater to him, to understand him in all his particular glory. (That's the heavy-lifting stuff when it comes to relationships, the grunt work, the stuff that has nothing to do with fun or great sex.)

Women, on the other hand, generally care for their lovers more than their husbands, but they'll stick with the person most likely to provide (either by choice or by court order) more resources in the long run.

That's why secrecy is a kindness. The truth, after all, is difficult to handle under the best of circumstances; most people would rather not know that they have fallen short in the reproductive, emotional, age, or looks sweepstakes and may be, at best, a compromise or even mercenary choice.

But when it comes to explaining this, it's easier to either stay faithful or not get caught in the first place. While the drive to mate with younger, better looking, more interesting, richer, or just different people makes perfect sense to the person enjoying the fruits of such a tryst, just try using this as an excuse for a discovered affair. The results will *not* be pretty.

Confess or Not?

A very wise person once said that the truth is not the first obligation of husbands and wives. Instead, the first obligation is to care about the other person, and a direct consequence of caring is a desire not to injure.

So, should you confess, either voluntarily or after being confronted with evidence of infidelity? There are three answers to that—*no, no,* and *no.* Confession may be good for the soul but not for the marriage, if you have any intention whatsoever of remaining in it. It causes pain for the person you may least want to injure (no, not yourself—your spouse!)

No moral slate is wiped clean by confessing, and the motivation to do so is self-serving at best. When an affair is confessed, it's usually the first one. Subsequent ones are concealed because you know better.

As mentioned above, men and women react differently as a general rule if forced to admit to an affair. Men fervently declare love for their affair partners, whereas women reject their lovers and implore the husband to realize that he is far superior (probably in the wallet department if not in the sack).

After all, protecting your turf is what it's all about. Women are afraid of losing their meal ticket, men their pride. Ultimately, however, tearful confessions and passionate pleas for a second chance will make you look like a fool. There's a certain pleasure one takes in groveling, but it's short-lived. The best way to deal with the pressure to confess is to avoid having to.

And don't jump the gun and admit to everything beforehand should a former lover threaten to tell your spouse all about your indiscretions. It could just be an idle threat to see how high you really *will* jump. So if you're found out, your best bet is to deny everything.

DENY, DENY, DENY

If your affair is discovered, *deny everything and demand proof.* If there is proof, deny that too. Why?

+ First, because begging for forgiveness creates a very bad precedent, and you don't ever want to give your spouse something to hold over you. He or she will, on a daily basis.

+ Second, because discovery can be a shattering event for the uninvolved spouse (although it shouldn't be), and the aftereffects can last a lifetime. There's no cure for what will surely be defined as betrayal.

+ Third, because it's really better that your social partner not know that your extramarital activities in the aggregate may have been a lot more satisfying and enjoyable than your marriage.

- Fourth, because conflict's a drag, and you have better things to do than to spend hours, days, or years listening to a litany of your shortcomings punctuated with shouts of "How could you do this to me?", to which you will be dying to reply, "Very easily."

- Fifth, because once you start you'll probably want to keep on having affairs. Do you really want your every movement and action scrutinized?

- Sixth, because this kind of marital hysteria is bad for your kids. You don't want them to become pawns in a gruesome power struggle that might result in genetic suicide due to abusive stepparents or a lowered standard of living.

- Seventh, because adultery is against the law in twenty-seven states and the District of Columbia—it can and will be used against you, and you'll be forced to pay and pay as a result of it.

- Finally, as we've said before, most people can't handle the truth. Denial allows spouses to keep both their illusions and a modicum of dignity. It also gives women in particular bragging rights as their friends' marriages crumble. In other words, your spouse really doesn't want to know, so don't tell.

The Intimacy Question

Once an affair is discovered or confessed to, the uninvolved spouse is generally counseled to confront the erring spouse in no uncertain terms. You, of course, will deny everything and resolve to be a hell of a lot more careful in the future.

But let's say your wife or husband rattles the truth out of you. One of the first questions put to a straying spouse usually goes as follows: "Is the thrill of the 'new' more important than the rewards of genuine intimacy with me?"

Talk about a loaded question!

People change. They grow together or apart, wander off (mentally or physically), and sometimes come back for a while to rest before their next foray. It isn't possible to know another person completely, nor should you want to.

Everyone—and that means you too—has the right to keep secrets in a mental space that remains inviolate. When women in particular desire more "intimacy" with you, what they want is admission to that secret space, mostly so that they can nag you incessantly about what they find there. Beyond a certain point, what someone else sees as an "invitation for intimacy" may be to you an invasion of privacy.

And people tend to overestimate the hold they have on their spouses anyway, whether or not any sort of intimacy has been achieved (and frankly, some people just aren't interesting enough to make delving into their "secret selves" worth the effort). The real hold is that of economics and children. Eliminate the child aspect in particular and you may be hanging by a thread, at least until you're both past reproductive age and the issue becomes more one of survival than love.

Romantic love fades fast, as we've seen. The only threads more fragile than those binding a childless marriage are those holding together an affair.

Love or Money?

It's not loss of love that gets women in particular all worked up when they discover their husbands cheating, but the potential loss of status and resources, either from divorce or having to share.

On the other hand, let your wife find a genuinely interested long-term prospect with better looks and more money than you have and—well. What percentage of married women do you think would leave their current relationships if they got a better offer from a better someone else? You probably can't count that high. A little cynicism is in order if your spouse tries to play the "love card" in an effort to make you feel guilty.

The Aftermath

There are plenty of books dealing with the aftermath of affairs. They usually contain all sorts of questionnaires about "your love IQ" and "feelings" and "intimacy and commitment," etc. Not only will they take hours to fill out, but they are also subject to interpretation by the last person you want passing judgment—your spouse.

Frankly, there is little anyone can do to bombproof a marriage against an affair. There's too much choice, too much mobility, just too much of everything out there to expect that the person in your life is going to remain faithfully at your side, or you at his or hers, for the next fifty years.

By the same token, married people who claim that they haven't been tempted to have an affair, even if they never followed through, are:

- So heinously unattractive or devoid of self-esteem that they're convinced they'll never find anyone else if they get caught; or,

- Completely dependent on their spouse as a source of supply; or,

- Lying.

For the vast majority of married people, fear guides affairs of the heart far more than love does. They don't want to lose their security, their social status, their home, their kids, or whatever tenuous hold they may have on a decent standard of living.

Sure it's easy to get comfortable within a marriage. To a certain degree, creating stability is the point of marriage, though too much stability can lead to fossilization. Even so, the domestic stuff that has been driving you up the wall can end up looking pretty good when you've lost custody of your kids and maybe wrecked your job prospects because of an affair that has gone public (though it's not an affair that you pursued at work—you know better than that now).

Even more so than a jilted lover, a jilted spouse can make life an ongoing hell for you. So if you can't bring yourself to get divorced, either stay faithful or don't get caught cheating.

CHAPTER 12

A FEW LAST THOUGHTS

*I*t's been said that people should marry three times: first for love, then for children, and finally for companionship. Some individuals can't find a single person able to successfully make the transition with them from phase to phase, so they seek out different partners through serial monogamy, marrying more than once.

Others do find that one very special person to journey with them, a person with an inborn knack for meeting and overcoming the radically different demands that each relationship phase—infatuation, reproduction and child care, and aging—puts on marriages. That one person not only brings the talents and qualities that serve to complete his or her beloved, but complements the beloved as he or she changes, a person ever responsive to need and nuance.

Frankly, that's not a marriage, that's a miracle, and if you are fortunate enough to have such a person in your life, the last thing you want to do is screw it up!

But most of us aren't that lucky. For us, adultery may have to suffice as a stand-in or proxy for serial marriage, a way to meet our changing needs and interests without formally severing the main social relationship we've been told should forever dominate our life.

Humans are contradictory creatures. We yearn for the old and the new simultaneously. Sometimes this means staying put, but sometimes it means using the boring but stable platform of marriage as a periodic launching pad for exploring other, more exciting options.

Fidelity Is Less Fun but Also Less Complicated

Knowing that both fidelity and infidelity are, at heart, reproductive strategies that can have little or nothing to do with "true love" or "soul mates" as we perceive them emotionally is the first step toward making rational decisions about your sexuality within marriage.

Being sexually and socially faithful is a hell of a lot less complicated. That boring and routine marriage can start looking awfully good when you're living in a one-bedroom apartment and struggling with an angry soon-to-be-ex, a lover who's demanding that the two of you get married, and possibly with onerous custody and support payments.

Lifelong marriage and sexual fidelity, while bitter pills to swallow, are human constructs that exist in large part to ensure that parents acknowledge and care for children. Frankly, your primary responsibility is not to your spouse, who has no excuse for naïveté in this day and age, but to the children who are already carrying your genetic banner. That responsibility may be best served by fidelity, because the opposite may cause them great distress.

Of course, if you're consciously interested in having more children (or any at all) with significantly different traits and characteristics, but want to remain in a committed relationship, then either serial marriage or affairs outside of your primary relationship are the only way to go.

But in the end it might be best for your overall genetic future (not to mention your finances) to remain faithful in every sense of the word, raising your children in tandem with the spouse who may turn out, fifty years down the road, to have been the best possible long-term choice—although by that time, it will be far too late to do anything about it if you chose poorly.

> **FUN ADULTERY FACT**
>
> *The winners in the genetic game we all play are those who choose correctly when it comes to reproductive and long-term survival strategies.*

Ultimately there's no right or wrong when it comes to having one affair or many. You'll base your decision on hunch, instinct, belief, desire, conscience, and emotion, overlaying a deeply unconscious desire for a reproductive "best."

If you can't have kids, or don't want them, or have as many as you want, it might be the height of folly to let your body and emotions push you into an extramarital relationship based on possible outcomes that you already know are unpalatable.

But there's always the possibility of meeting just the right lover who'll save you from genetic extinction (or maybe emotional or relational extinction if kids aren't on the agenda). And affairs can keep marriages intact by helping you release the emotional and sexual pressure that may be driving you to seek a divorce in the first place. These are possibilities worth exploring.

The Choice Is Always Yours

Whether a marriage or an affair, your relationships will run through the same basic life cycle: infatuation, attachment, disillusion, and dissolution. Some couples, thanks to their chemical or emotional or personality makeup, will manage to stay "in love" forever, with no desire to seek other options outside their marriage. Most of us, however, aren't that lucky.

If it's in your reproductive, social, and financial best interests to stay with your current spouse, then chances are you will. But it's absurd to think that a decision you made in your early twenties, to stay emotionally and sexually faithful to one person for the rest of your life, is going to still look good when you're forty.

"Opportunity cost" is a concept that applies as much to real life as it does to economics. How many other opportunities—for a happier life or better, more successful kids or a better lifestyle—are you forgoing by remaining faithful? Of course, it works the other way too. How many opportunities—to watch your kids grow, to age gracefully and well with someone who truly cares for you—have you thrown away with both hands by running around?

Ultimately most humans are dynamic. They want and need forward motion. If no such movement is taking place in the marriage then it will be taking place elsewhere, by way of intellectual or sexual couplings with compatible individuals meeting specific needs of the moment. To think otherwise is naïve in the extreme.

THE RULES OF AFFAIRS

1. **Don't get caught.**

2. **Safe sex, please.**

3. **Observe the 50-Mile Rule.**

4. **Choose lovers wisely.**

5. **Compartmentalize your relationships.**

6. **Lay out the ground rules first thing.**

7. **No wholesale changes in your look or lifestyle.**

8. **Keep communication with your lover to a minimum.**

9. **Be honest but not open.**

10. **Don't take affairs personally.**

11. **Make no promises.**

12. **Keep your affairs secret.**

13. **Keep your children out of your sex life.**

14. **Money and gifts are a trap.**

15. **Know when they're onto you.**

16. **Know when to call it quits.**

17. **End each affair as graciously as you can.**

18. **If discovered—deny, deny, deny.**

19. **Revenge is not an option.**

20. **Don't feel guilty.**

RULE #1: *Don't get caught*

The decision to reveal an affair should be yours and yours alone. It should be made consciously and in your own good time, if *you* feel like doing so, not because someone else forces you to.

There's very little upside to having an affair come out into the open. Occasionally such a revelation leads to a reexamination and strengthening of the marriage, but the improvement is usually only temporary and achieved only at the expense of a lot of yelling, shrieking, and endless recrimination. Who needs the aggravation?

And once you're dinged, the suspicion is always there. Women in particular have radar, or think they do. (And spouses in general, male and female, have looooooooooooong memories when it comes to this kind of thing.) Even if you're "forgiven" for your indiscretions, your misery quotient will go up exponentially. Getting caught is simply not worth it.

If you feel that you can't get out of or ultimately don't *want* out of your marriage, fine. But don't act in word or deed around your spouse or in public as if you were free, and take care that your lover doesn't force you into making a decision you shouldn't have to make. Choose your lovers well, be discreet, and use common sense.

As we've seen, affairs are undertaken as part of your secret self, and you have every right to keep that secret *to* yourself. It's possible to operate ethically within two spheres, and that of course should be the goal. Your marriage and your affairs should have nothing to do with one another. Keep them separate and unrelated, no matter what—or who—tempts you to do otherwise.

RULE #2: *Safe sex, please*

Despite medical advances, there are plenty of sexually transmitted diseases (STDs) out there, none of which you'll want to bring home or spread. Even though you'll deny being the cause (see Rule #18), you'll get a queasy feeling on the day that your spouse comes home and says that she or he has herpes and how could that be?

STDs are serious business. They can kill. They can also cause infertility, and surely you don't want your genetic hopes dashed because of something you contracted during a one-night gene exchange or recreational sexual blow-out. Nor do you want the lawsuit your lover might bring against you for passing something on to him or her.

And let's not forget the dangers of an undesired pregnancy. Getting pregnant is a time-honored way of forcing the divorce issue. You cannot just assume that your lover is using contraception.

Remember—affairs come into being because you want sex, and you want sex due to deeply unconscious reproductive drives. Maybe you aren't thinking in terms of reproductive options, but that doesn't mean your lover isn't. You might be that person's last, best hope of fending off genetic suicide.

DNA testing and child-support laws have made proving paternity—and extracting payment—much easier. For millions of years guys could pretty much "hit and run," but those days are over. For that matter, so are the days when a woman could just assume that her husband would accept every child as his own. Even a simple blood test could rock your world.

So follow the safe sex guidelines: use condoms and birth control. Choose your partners with care and try to uncover their hidden agendas. Don't become a pawn in someone else's reproductive game.

RULE #3: *Observe the 50-Mile Rule*

Your lover and your spouse shouldn't live—or work—within fifty miles of each other. They should *never* have any reason to come into contact with each other for any reason at any time. The only connection between them is you, and you keep Marriage World and Affair World separate at all times.

Offices, health clubs, and school activities bring people together constantly. Work in particular seems to breed romance. People are thrown into close contact with each other, have similar interests, and often a lot in common. When people have office affairs, it's because they're convenient and intellectually engaging.

They're also stupid for innumerable reasons. It's almost impossible to keep up a façade of dispassionate, professional interest and normalcy when having an affair with a coworker. When the affair ends, coming into contact with that person every day will be excruciating and dangerous. The only more foolish way to conduct an affair is to do so within the social circle you share with your spouse.

Men in particular have a bad habit of wanting to bring wives and lovers together socially, as a form of ego fulfillment. After all, while many men don't have the love of even one woman, here you are with two! Body language alone will give you away.

The far-away-from-home affair is the only smart choice. By definition your involvement is limited. This way, you don't reveal too much about yourself, and that helps prevent genuine attachment. A person you see all the time either socially or in a work environment is going to know waaaaaay too much about you—and your family and lifestyle—for comfort.

The away-from-home affair also prevents you from using your lover's house or your own as a trysting place. Sure it's convenient, but think it through—your lover must park the car so that the neighbors don't see, then get into the house. Then he or she will have to hide if the kids come home early, or if someone knocks on the door. Conniving lovers can leave personal belongings lying around. Dirty sheets can get left behind (just perfect for that new do-it-yourself sperm-testing kit). And why should any outsider know the layout of your house?

Statistically, the most popular place to engage in extramarital sex is the woman's home, then the man's, then cars, a friend's place, the office, or a park. How absurd! How undignified! Fumbling around in the backseat of a car or in a grove of bushes was a hell of a lot more fun when you were twenty. Stick to out-of-town hotels, and don't leave anything behind that could end up in a big care package addressed to your spouse.

RULE #4: *Choose lovers wisely*

You must always remember that no matter how short or long the affair, a lover will forever remain your partner in deception. This is a heavy responsibility indeed to lay on someone whom you barely know, or even want to know.

The mechanisms by which we choose whom to love appear random, but it's becoming increasingly apparent through research that they are anything but. Make sure that you are attracting—and taking—as a lover the kind of person who will not only meet your sexual and emotional needs, but who will keep your secrets. Because, in an odd sort of way, you're asking a more or less total stranger to adhere more faithfully to you than you are to your lifelong mate.

RULE #5: *Compartmentalize your relationships*

Compartmentalization is the key to guiltless affairs. Learn to feel comfortable in those worlds we call Marriage World and Affair World. Each has its own requirements and obligations; each allows you a separate emotional identity and the chance to explore different sides of your personality.

At the same time, however, you must be able to move between your lives naturally and comfortably. Guilt appears when they overlap, and problems of discovery often occur when you let them merge without a neutral zone in between.

Keep your affairs clean and separate. Live them intensely when you're with your lover, and put thoughts of them aside when you're not (admittedly a far easier task if you've chosen your lover wisely). Compartmentalization is a key aspect to keeping your affairs secret, as they should be.

RULE #6: *Lay out the ground rules first thing*

Laying out the ground rules for an affair is just like putting together a prenuptial agreement, with the exception that whatever you agree to isn't legally binding (neither are some prenups for that matter). In an affair, you're betting to a great degree that faith, trust, and affection will trump anger or the desire for revenge when the time comes to call it quits.

Of course, the start of any affair is a heady time. You're confused over what you're feeling, a little dismayed at the intensity of it all, and worried that maybe your marriage truly *is* at risk because you've maybe found the person you've been practicing for. The last thing you want to do is rock the boat by implying that there are practical issues that must be dealt with before the fun begins.

Nevertheless, one of the things that successful affairs have in common is an understanding on the part of both parties exactly where the relationship fits into their everyday lives, and agreement as to where it might lead, if anywhere. And while the married person generally holds the whip hand—as the person whose schedule generally takes precedence—the lover must be an equal partner here, with equal understanding of the rules and the right to fashion them.

Some rules, as we've seen, should be inviolate, such as:

- No communication whatsoever to your house
- No contact with spouse or kids
- No gooey e-mails, faxes, phone calls to the office
- No interference or presence in each other's lives beyond Affair World

It's at this point too that married partners must state unequivocally that they have no intention of divorcing if that's indeed the case. Dishonesty here can lead to big problems down the road.

As it is, if one lover is unattached, he or she is going to be harboring secret thoughts about marriage anyway, even if he or she never gets up the nerve to say so to your face. You must nip this one in the bud immediately. In affairs as in life, *everyone has an agenda.* Chances are your lover's agenda has little to do with yours, since the reproductive and emotional needs of men and women (and marrieds and singles) are diametrically opposed to one another. Just because someone is a lover and not a spouse doesn't alter that fact.

As the relationship goes through the various stages we've seen— infatuation, attachment, disillusion, and dissolution—it must occasionally be renegotiated, and the ground rules revised or reiterated. Once an affair reaches the attachment stage, that feeling of comfort and general well-being can spill over to your real life. That's a no-no.

So take care to renegotiate the ground rules periodically. Private misunderstandings sometimes have an unfortunate way of becoming public disasters.

RULE #7: *No wholesale changes in your look or lifestyle*

The middle-aged guy frantically trying to make himself over— hair transplants, manicures, jogging, health club—has become a national joke. Women, of course, can be utterly obsessed with their looks, but it's still not quite acceptable for men.

Maybe you wake up one day and realize that you're paunchy and out of shape, that ten years of marriage have made you fat and sloppy. You decide to try and recapture your lost youth. Fine, as far as that goes. But these kinds of changes—weight loss, more interest in clothes and fashion, plastic surgery, and the like—can be a red flag to your spouse indicating that you're in an affair or are considering one.

If getting back into shape or learning Russian or changing careers is part of your approach to getting or keeping a lover, go for it. Just be sure to position what you're doing carefully. Remember that even less blatant indicators can be detected by an observant spouse, things like:

- Living a more independent life
- Withdrawing from the family or becoming too attentive
- Buying gifts when you're normally forgetful
- Complaining about life at home constantly, or ceasing to complain
- A lack of interest in sex, renewed interest, or a sudden interest in novel new positions
- Better grooming, fitness
- Suspicious phone calls, quick hang-ups, furtive conversations
- Changed passenger seat adjustments in the car
- New soaps or smells
- Too clean when coming home from work/trip

◆ Unusual phone/cell phone/computer bills

◆ Extra key on key ring

◆ Excuses to go out alone at night

◆ Inability to ejaculate during sex (it can sometimes take hours to recharge, and traces of a lover can remain for hours)

◆ Little lies and omissions

◆ A new interest in becoming a summer bachelor while the family vacations elsewhere

◆ New reading or listening habits; mentions of movies and plays you didn't see with your spouse

◆ Striped ties that get reconfigured during the day

◆ Following a new astrological sign

◆ Using new slang and lingo

◆ Calling your spouse by the wrong name

When you're all caught up in the pleasures of Affair World, it's sometimes difficult to remember that things on the home front must remain the same—but you forget this to your peril.

RULE # 8: *Keep communication with your lover to a minimum*

Love affairs by definition lend themselves to endless protestations of love and affection—that's why they're called "love affairs" and not "business affairs." In any event, everyone likes to receive letters and cards and those "just thinking of you" phone calls and e-mails. However, the place to indulge yourself is face to face, not at home while your spouse is sitting in the other room playing Candyland with the kids. More errant spouses have been caught because of letters left lying around and hasty phone calls than any other reasons combined. (Here's a phrase that should strike terror in your heart—Caller ID.)

If you commit your thoughts to paper—or to the ether that is e-mail—just remember that love letters are both tangible and traceable, and great ammunition for use by jilted lovers. If you must send letters and cards, don't sign them. If you can't bear to destroy the ones you get back, find an imaginative place to hide them (women tend to hide them in lingerie drawers, men in file cabinets).

Ideally, your lover shouldn't have your home address, home phone, fax, pager, primary e-mail address, or cell phone number. Get a P.O. box and keep the key in your office. Use a false address when you get the box so that no mail will be inadvertently forwarded to your home, and get the box in a location *other* than your local post office.

Prepaid phone cards are useful in keeping incriminating phone numbers off your home bill, but have an excuse for having one if your spouse asks. If you can't memorize your lover's phone number, then write it down without the area code (another great reason to observe the 50-Mile Rule).

If you and your lover call each other at work, use nicknames so that your identity stays private. Choosing nicknames can be a playful and evocative form of sex play. Use these names religiously when calling each other. And don't leave legitimate return phone numbers—your secretary may be a spy on your spouse's team.

A word on electronics—we have entered a brave new world of communication. So far as your love affairs are concerned, keep your trips down the information superhighway to a bare minimum. There is absolutely nothing private about e-mail for example, at home or at work; your password can be breached, and your employer has the right to look at whatever messages you send or receive at the office. A whimsical "I love you" translated by alpha-numeric pager can be intercepted by the wrong person, and cell-phone scanners are available at any Radio Shack for under a hundred bucks.

For that matter, the Internet has opened up a whole universe of surveillance and tracking capabilities. With just your social security number, and sometimes not even that, a disgruntled spouse or lover can get information on your credit and mail order history, current or past employment, travel preferences, criminal or military records, and yes, your home address and private phone numbers. Nothing is really private these days . . . all the more reason to choose your affair partners wisely and to reveal as little about your real life as possible from the start.

RULE #9: *Be honest but not open*

That people will do just about anything for sex and affection is a well-known fact. Common deceptions include saying you're single when you're not in order to bed someone who might otherwise turn you down. Some people manage to pull off this deception for years because they don't want to go to the trouble of finding and romancing a new lover, so they lead the unattached partner on—all well and good, until your marital status is somehow revealed.

This kind of deception goes well beyond rotten—it stinks. It's this kind of blatant disregard for someone who may care for you very much that has a tendency to turn around and bite you right back.

But even being honest about your marital status doesn't absolve you if you create false expectations. Maybe your wife *doesn't* understand you, and maybe you *haven't* had sex for years, but saying so to a gullible lover creates false hopes that can lead to real problems down the road.

There's a significant difference between being honest and being open. To be honest means to share right from the beginning both your marital status and your goals for the affair. If you have no intention of getting a divorce, it's better to say so from the start.

And at the start is the time for the unattached person to also state his or her own goals. So anxious are some single women in particular to enter into a relationship of any sort that they'll give any answer you want, but if marriage and kids are actually a part of their game plan, you'd better ferret it out in advance.

Being honest, however, does *not* mean being open about your real life. It doesn't mean sharing secrets with your affair partner, on the assumption that this is a purer form of love, based on emotion and not economics. It does *not* mean that you discuss your marital, child, or business problems. It does *not* mean that you seek out the kind of intimacy you've been avoiding with your spouse.

Avoiding openness is a tough one. Whatever the tangle of drives leading you into an affair, one of the true pleasures of maintaining a physical and emotional relationship with someone other than your spouse is just that potential for sharing, for unburdening yourself, for getting another opinion, or simply getting validation of your worth as an individual, as opposed to being just a dad, or a wife, or an ATM. Any love affair worthy of the name—and certainly any shadow marriage—has a deeply emotional context. It must, or it wouldn't be worth pursuing.

But . . . an affair is a calculated risk at best. You should never give your lover an excess of ammunition to use against you should the relationship go south. Remember when you were courting your spouse, how you fixated on every little thing she or he told you?

Well, your lover could just as easily be fixating too. In the beginning, of course, you take delight in sharing little bits of truth.

Sometimes they pour out in a rush, so excited are you at the chance to unburden yourself. These details are all a part of the wonder of you, and so worthy of attention. Your lover takes pleasure in being such a worthy listener, all cuddled up in bed and basking in that postcoital glow.

It's just these little details, however, that will often come back to haunt you later. First, they can serve as hard-to-deny evidence that a person who claims to be your lover is indeed just that. Second, the intimate nature of such revelations gives the lover false hope for the future.

So spare yourself future trouble and embarrassment. Be honest about your marital status and the hopes you have for the affair. Within Affair World, you are a different person, able to show off different aspects of your personality, and to an adoring audience at that. Confine your conversation and philosophizing to issues involving Affair World alone.

RULE #10: *Don't take affairs personally*

Long-term love in all its chemical glory coupled with an ideal reproductive relationship is a thing so rare it's hard to imagine that it exists. Of course it does, for a few lucky people. The rest of us must either compromise over time or continue the search. And as we've seen, both strategies are fraught with risk.

In the end, women get the best man their looks can attract, and men get the best woman their resources can hold. The fact that looks and resources change over time is one reason among others why "love" can be so mercenary.

Compromise too much in your choice of mate and you may be saddled with inferior children and an inferior lifestyle. Keep looking too long and you may never find a better person with whom to mate. Infidelity broadens your options, which is how it serves the needs of both the married person seeking variety and the single person seeking any reproductive outlet at all.

It is the fortunate person who finds another who fits his or her love map to a "T," and whose chemical makeup is such that attachment may last a lifetime. Most of us, however, will find that any number of people fit our love maps. The first person we find who meets minimally acceptable criteria and doesn't blow us off is often the person we marry.

But that doesn't mean that there aren't a hundred other acceptable candidates out there, whose paths we may cross as time goes by. Given a certain set of circumstances, any of these other candidates could well become affair material.

In other words, since "love" is chemically induced and often transitory, it can be a highly impersonal thing. With time it may take on a "my one and only" element, but that's precisely *because* you've invested time in the relationship. There may be lots of other people with whom you might have bonded equally as well, or poorly, or better, but you picked this one to spend time with.

So much of life is timing, and that's as true of affairs as it is of anything else. The person who gets there first, the person with prior claim—the spouse, in other words—has gotten a head start on knowing and dealing with you, and that's a difficult advantage for a lover to overcome. Nearly impossible, as a matter of fact.

This is why you must never take affairs personally. Every person in a romantic relationship starts out as a "type," not an individual. Only with time does that change, and few affairs, even shadow marriages, have that luxury.

Enjoy your extramarital adventures, have fun with them, and revel in the little worlds that you create. But realize that although you're with this particular person right now, it could have been any number of people with similar characteristics. To say that lovers are interchangeable isn't true exactly, but what a lover is, is replaceable, much more so than a spouse, with whom there are far more legal entanglements.

Affairs provide an illusory sense of freedom, the chance to explore without commitment the many roads not taken. At any point, lovers may reach a fork in the road in the form of a new person with an even more alluring set of possibilities than the previous lover possesses. Without the legal and prior claims that chafe and bind, affair partners are free to take off, often with few or no regrets.

So keep your affairs impersonal. You can do this best by observing the 50-Mile Rule and not dealing with people with whom you have a social relationship.

RULE #11: *Make no promises*

Never make a significant promise to your lover. The fewer you make, the fewer you'll need to break. Never make statements like "You changed my life" or "Before I met you my life was nothing." Maybe you mean the statement at the time. Maybe you sincerely feel that your current lover is the light of your life. But these are the statements that lovers hold onto while you're back home coaching your kid's t-ball team, and these are the statements that come back to haunt.

Along the same lines, never tell your true fantasies to a lover, who can easily see him- or herself as the person residing on that boat during the round-the-world cruise, or the person sharing coffee with you while you putter around the garden at the little cabin by the lake. A married person's outside relationships are usually subsidies to the marriage, not substitutes for it, and whatever words are spoken in the heat of passion are just that, words. But words feed hopes and dreams, often unrealistically and to no good end.

RULE #12: *Keep your affairs secret*

The old saying goes that once two people know a secret, it's no longer a secret. This is even more true of affairs than it is of anything else.

There are lots of ways affairs can be revealed: car accidents, a chance meeting with a coworker, getting sick while with your lover, an inopportune phone call, getting slapped with a paternity suit or a claim that you spread an STD. This is part of the risk you take on when you play around. For some people, the risk is the best part of the deal. They get a charge out of the adventure aspect, the feeling that they're walking a tightrope with disaster looming on each side. Secrecy enhances that adventurous feeling.

Infatuation and attachment can lead anyone to do some pretty stupid things. You may want to flaunt your new relationship and show it off to the world, sometimes right under your spouse's nose. Affairs are ego boosts for men, and feed directly into women's vanity. To be "chosen" is a delightful feeling on any level, to be chosen for your reproductive possibilities is more delightful still, and to be chosen despite great personal risk can be positively transcendent.

But affairs should be kept secret. They are a hidden part of your life and should be kept that way. What, ultimately, is the point of making such a relationship public knowledge? Revenge, mostly.

After all, hate is the flipside of love. We hate that upon which we are most dependent. Often in your married life you may truly feel the need to take revenge on your spouse, who annoys you daily with his or her very presence, neediness, and endless demands. You're certain you could have done better—maybe you could have.

But ultimately, you're the one who made the decision to marry and take on the responsibilities that came along with it, including kids. And even though affairs offer opportunities that can serve to make your marriage tolerable over the long run, you still have to deal with a situation at home that's very much of your own making.

That's why you are under obligation to keep Affair World hidden. Exposing your extramarital activities will do nothing but hurt your kids and make you vulnerable to a host of indignities, such as having your spouse keep track of your every move or—shudder—having to give up half your income. Who needs it?

In short, be discreet, not only because it's fun but because it's necessary. Not everyone in the outside world is going to share your joy at the new love you've found, and the payment extracted for your happiness may be far greater than you are willing to pay.

RULE #13: *Keep your children out of your sex life*

It's a truly odd aspect of human nature that we spend so much time jockeying for the best genetic position but often treat the resulting children with such indifference. It takes years and years to teach kids how to function in the modern world, and yet our bodies and emotions often want to adhere to the ancient patterns that saw just getting kids through infancy as the main responsibilities of a parent.

In the distant past, when our ancestors were perfecting the physiological patterns that are still manifest in our modern lives, children were cared for very differently. Life was infinitely more communal, tied together by blood, necessity, and lack of geographic mobility. The economic and social burdens of child rearing were shared across the tribe or the group, which had a big investment both in genetic variety and in protecting its collective heritage.

But in the modern world, the nuclear family is the unit responsible for raising kids, and while the government offers assistance, it takes more in taxes than it gives back in help. Nuclear families have some true disadvantages over the ancient forms.

Responsibilities that used to be spread across a range of aunts, grandparents, cousins, and the like are now shared by just two overburdened parents with finite resources. The more kids you have with the same person, the fewer resources are available for each child individually. There's no economic replenishment from outside sources, the type a woman might expect if she had kids by a variety of men. (Of course, those men could also just hit and run, leaving the woman with no alternative but to try and cuckold her existing husband into believing the little darlings are his.)

In any event, creating a child with a lover is not a rational act in today's world, if you plan to keep the parentage hidden. Married people wishing to avoid big-time trouble avoid conception outside of marriage, period. It's better to try your hand at true serial monogamy by way of divorce with all the problems that it creates, particularly for your existing kids.

For the most part, stepparents have no particular need to honor your genetic contribution to the world. "Blended families" may be here to stay, but before you embark on a great love affair that may change the very foundation of the first family that you created, ask yourself whether you honestly believe that your existing genetic heritage, as embodied in your children, would be better entrusted to someone else. If you don't, then act with discretion at the very least.

Reproductive one-upmanship is a game for adults, and sometimes the uninvolved spouse deserves little sympathy or special consideration when an affair comes to light. Married people often greatly overestimate the emotional and physical hold they have on their spouses and take their relationships very much for granted.

But the children you produce are a special responsibility. It is your obligation to shield them from the world's miseries—something with which they will become acquainted soon enough—and among those miseries is the aftermath of a discovered affair. Don't put them in the middle of your battles with your spouse, don't introduce them to your newest squeeze, and don't make them pawns in whatever battle of attrition you may be fighting. They deserve better. After all, they're carrying *your* genetic torch.

RULE #14: *Money and gifts are a trap*

It's true—money is the greatest aphrodisiac around. There's nothing like it to draw a crowd, no matter what you look like. Even short guys look better when they stand on their wallets, and having money is pretty much mandatory when it comes to managing an affair.

Since you are strictly following the 50-Mile Rule and restricting your trysts to out-of-town locations, you'll need a hotel room, entertainment, dining, and travel money. And you'll need these things over and above whatever regular expenses you need to provide for your family. Affairs are for fun after all, and money makes for fun.

Gifts are as much a part of Affair World as they are of Marriage World. Lovers should acknowledge each other during holidays and birthdays, particularly since the married partner will never be available during those times, which is often sad for the unattached. If it's a love affair, secrecy doesn't absolve you from thoughtfulness (although sentiment doesn't absolve you from being cautious either).

But gifts should be well thought out. It's never a good idea to give expensive jewelry to anyone other than your spouse, but if you must, don't engrave it with your initials and promises of eternal fealty. Don't give some transient romantic object family heirlooms either. (Don't snicker—it happens.)

Gift certificates to places like record, book, or video stores make good presents for the married partner since there's nothing out of the ordinary about such purchases, and he or she won't need to explain where a certain article of clothing or jewelry came from.

Just stay away from elaborate presents that raise suspicions, and by all means don't put things on your charge cards. Not only can a charge to, say, a jewelry store, raise a red flag if your spouse hasn't seen any gifts lately, but charging something often leads to being put on a mailing list, and you don't need such catalogs coming to your house.

RULE #15: *Know when they're onto you*

How do you know when your spouse is on to you? Here are some clues:

- He or she changes weekend plans at the last minute, so that your plans to be with your lover are thrown off.

- Friends are invited over "spontaneously" to keep you occupied.

- Your family—or your spouse's—is invited for a long stay.

- Your spouse initiates a "family hour" every evening.

- Your spouse starts popping in at the house during the day, calls you at odd hours at work.

◆ Your spouse borrows money at the spur of the moment so that you're late for your date.

◆ Your spouse takes an interest in phone and credit card bills that he or she never cared about, or starts checking the mail, or starts looking at e-mail and the site history on your computer far more carefully.

◆ Your spouse changes his or her sex patterns.

Vigilance is the watchword here. If you suspect your spouse is onto you, cool it with your lover for the time being, or end the relationship altogether. But don't try to compensate by seeming totally reenergized or recommitted to your marriage when such wasn't the case before the affair. That's a red flag too.

RULE #16: *Know when to call it quits*

An affair or shadow marriage has reached the end when the effort to keep it going outweighs the benefits received. Often one person reaches this conclusion independent of the other—unilaterally, in other words. He or she gets bored, or scared, or finds someone new. The old lover has lost that unconscious genetic appeal.

Once you're ready to bail, the trick is to get out without hurting or pissing off your lover to the extent that he or she might want to wreak vengeance on you, and before they try to force the issue themselves.

How might your soon-to-be ex-lover do that? Well, in a bid to change the ground rules, your lover may start leaving tell-tale marks—scratches, hickeys, perfume residue, lipstick—in obvious places. Or he or she starts asking about the divorce you promised, and will no longer be put off by whatever vague assurances you manage to mumble. Maybe your own marriage is such a mess that you've forgotten why people marry in the first place but trust us, your lover (particularly if she's a single woman) will have the facts right at hand.

A married person, even if a dolt, has status in our society. By definition, since they're married, someone at one time or another saw value in them. The single person doesn't have that sanction. Though few singles care to admit it, to be unmarried is often equated with being unwanted and so a failure at life's most basic yet important relationship.

Add to this issues of long-term financial security and kids, and it's easy to see why even bad marriages are often considered better than none, and why some lovers will stop at nothing to get you to sign on the dotted line.

Of course, once a lover starts trying to put his or her "mark" on you, either literally or figuratively, or pointedly refuses to adhere to the guidelines set early in the relationship, it's past time to get out. But even if nothing traumatic has happened, you may just want to move on and be done with it. Whatever the case, know when to call it quits, but do so as gently and as tactfully as you can. Here's where keeping things impersonal will pay real dividends.

RULE #17: *End each affair as graciously as you can*

It's rare for affairs and shadow marriages to end well. After all, the emotions are still there, and needs that may have been met will now be going unfulfilled. As a general rule, it's easier for men to call it quits than it is for women. For the reasons we've already seen, men just don't get as attached, and they often have less trouble latching onto someone else than women do.

Sure, when you want out, you want *out*. But think about things from your lover's point of view. This person is also risking something by being with you, even if it's only self-respect (although a cynic might say that, if he or she could find someone of their own, they wouldn't be dealing with you anyway).

Here's a person who has tasted of happiness and wants more. Just because you get bored or get a conscience or get found out or find someone new, doesn't mean that your lover will relinquish you that easily. He or she may have transmogrified your interest into the one shining aspect of life, not to mention their one shot at a reproductive future. And while this person may not mean that much to you, you may mean a great deal to them. If you've unwisely shared too much information about yourself, the stage has been set for an ugly confrontation.

So don't take a cavalier attitude when it comes to bringing things to an end. Once you've left your lover behind, there's utterly no incentive, beyond respect and lingering affection for you, to keep your secrets. And respect and lingering affection can be fleeting sentiments indeed.

RULE #18: *If discovered—deny, deny, deny*

Ah, Jack Nicholson. Remember that great scene in *A Few Good Men* when he roared "You can't handle the truth!"?

Well, most people, married people in particular, can't. The spouse who accuses you of having an affair, in his or her heart of hearts, really doesn't want a confirmation. They want denial, because this keeps intact the public façade of a happy, or at least workable, marriage—a marriage, by the way, that may be in your spouse's best reproductive and/or financial interests, if not in yours.

So do yourself and everyone around you a favor. Memorize Rule #1 and act accordingly. But if for some reason you do get nailed . . .

Deny everything and demand proof.

If proof is forthcoming, deny that too. Photos, tapes, a printed history of your forays to Internet porn sites . . . just about any evidence can be digitally created, enhanced, or fabricated these days. In fact, deny involvement even if your spouse catches you in the act.

We've already heard the old joke where a wife walks in on her husband in bed with another woman. As the wife goes to leave in a huff, the man implores her to reconsider, saying, "Who are you going to believe—your own eyes or me?" He's got the right idea.

Because, after all, what does confession lead to but recrimination, anger, hurt, rage, sexual frustration, sometimes months or years of expensive therapy, and lifelong distrust? Your spouse doesn't want to know that you live in two worlds, and that he or she takes precedence only in one, meaning that he or she isn't the center of your universe. Your spouse certainly doesn't want to know that the concept of opportunity cost—the opportunities you're forgoing by staying with him or her—may be a factor in the decision to seek out a better bet.

Admitting to an affair almost always leads to nothing but misery. It can make a bad situation infinitely worse. Do everything you can (short of physical harm) to avoid the need to do so.

RULE #19: *Revenge is not an option*

When a lover leaves you behind, the desire to destroy him or her can be overwhelming. And of course, the easiest way to do so is to take on the uninvolved spouse. After all, what better way to extract revenge, than to make your ex-lover's home life a living hell?

A delightful thought, but one that should remain just that, a thought. Whether or not you went into the affair with your eyes open, whether or not you realized that your lover was married, there's little to be gained from screwing over a person you once genuinely cared for. You've been left behind. It hurts, and it's unfair, maybe even devastating, but it's reality.

So forget about the midnight hang-up calls to the spouse, the stalking, the nasty letters to the conniving creep's kids, boss, parents. There's indeed a delicious aspect to calling up turncoat's spouse or new lover and saying, "He loves me more than he loves you." Maybe he does. But making that call isn't going to bring him back to you.

And don't threaten to kill yourself or do bodily harm to someone else. There's no point in creating some sort of drama in which you're the star, because nothing is going to send your ex-lover back to her or his spouse faster, and nothing will bring two people together faster than having to confront this kind of situation. *You lose.*

So forget revenge. Pour your rage, anger, and frustration into a letter. Call the lover who so callously abandoned you (in direct violation of Rule #17) every name in the book. Promise to inflict the most diabolical tortures in all the most sensitive places. Enjoy these torments as many times as you want to by way of the written word. Then burn the letter, or delete it. Just don't send it.

Your rage and hurt are real, but these feelings do fade. There probably is someone else out there for you. Spend your time more profitably looking for that person, instead of mooning over someone who's gone.

And remember, as a wise person said, "Time wounds all heels." Ex-lovers generally get theirs somewhere down the road.

RULE #20: *Don't feel guilty*

Guilt and shame are the emotions that are "supposed" to accompany adultery. Baloney! Legal standing has nothing to do with the rightness or wrongness of your actions. Guilt is something that has been transmitted from one generation to the next, in part to secure obedience against reproductive chaos. Mostly this had to do with not violating another man's property, period.

When a man feels guilty, it shows that he is thinking only of himself. He is staging an act in which he is both cast and audience. If he's really thinking of his spouse, he'll do nothing to shatter the illusion of faithfulness she's content to cling to. In other words, maintain that illusion and there's nothing to feel guilty about.

Women, on the other hand, even today, often have a terror of the outside world and look to men to provide security. They feel guilty only when that security is threatened by discovery.

Remember, the harm isn't in the infidelity itself, but in what happens afterward. Treat spouse, lover, and children with kindness and consideration, and watch guilt disappear.

A Special Note...for Single Women Involved in an Affair

Each single woman comes by her "singlehood" differently. Sometimes it's by choice, sometimes by chance, such as divorce or death. Or maybe she's never come across a corresponding love map. Unrequited love may be the only kind she's ever known.

Whatever the case may be, single women still have the same reproductive and emotional needs everyone else has. They want to love and be loved, even if love is fleeting as we've seen. Few people choose to be alone, and no one wants to be considered inconsequential, which is the status that society confers on the unattached.

Women in particular have a problem in this regard. It's estimated that millions of American women at any given time will have no mate, simply because there aren't enough marriageable, appropriate men to go around. Yet no amount of sermonizing from the pulpit or feminist cant is going to make celibacy or childlessness acceptable to a woman who wants a traditional family structure but has no relationship within which to begin one.

So, for a goodly number of women—maybe you—an affair can be a source of love and emotional and sexual support, maybe the only source. Even as a compromise choice, a married lover can be better than no lover at all. Such a liaison may prove your only chance to play out your own reproductive game plan.

It's easy to see why single women often invest too much emotion and commitment to adulterous relationships. Whatever your sole source of succor is, it is going to take center stage in your life, a point that your married lover will either forget or manage to use against you, even if he really is a nice guy.

Remember—the sexual and emotional benefits of one-night stands, sporadic affairs, and even shadow marriages are only supplements to the benefits your lover is already getting in marriage. And, contrary to what he might say, these benefits can be substantial.

So though you may see an affair as a shiny substitute for a relationship with genuine, long-term potential, it's a poor substitute indeed—and in your heart of hearts, you probably know it. In the long run, it will probably avail you nothing anyway. Only about 5 percent of men divorce to marry their lovers, and such marriages rarely last.

Add to this misery the adversarial position men and women have in general with regard to their reproductive and emotional needs, and it's easy to see why the interests of both parties in a single—married extramarital relationship can be diametrically opposed to one another. At base, affairs exist to create new reproductive opportunities, but a bonus child with you or anyone else for that matter, is probably the last thing any rational married man wants.

So, it's sad but true—a man with a long-time spouse, a home, and maybe children, a career and heavy financial obligations is simply not going to chuck it all for you and your one-bedroom condo, no matter what he may say or wish to the contrary. The law of prior claim applies here and the spouse has it. Accept this and act accordingly.

Single women must always enter into new relationships with their eyes (as opposed to their legs) wide open. Men will do just about anything for sex, sometimes crying piteously about the horrors of married life, sometimes claiming to be single, all in an effort to get you into bed for a quick recreational tryst. Awful as it sounds, cynicism can play a big role in your being "chosen," cynicism as in "desperate" and "available."

Even when some great guy claiming to be single starts dating up a storm with you, evidence may point to the contrary—he won't give you a live phone number, you never go to his house, he's out of town a lot (in other words, he's following the advice in this book). Things just don't develop in a logical way. When the truth about his marital status comes out—and it will—you could easily be devastated, blinded by your own wishful thinking.

Generally, however, a married man with a yen for you, or your general type, is going to state his status straight out. It's at this point that you need to make a decision. If the perceived benefits of living in Affair World for a while don't outweigh the inevitable hurt, then decline the invitation, keep your mouth shut, and leave it at that.

If you choose to go ahead, however, you must then adhere to the ground rules—complete discretion, cooperation, and consideration. This means minimal contact when you're not together, following his schedule even if it conflicts with yours, no sharing of the relationship with family and friends, safe sex and contraception (ironic but necessary), and above all, a willingness to keep the relationship secret forever, no matter how much the inevitable parting hurts, or how badly he bungles it.

The decision to end an affair is often made unilaterally, generally by the very person who initiated it in the first place—the married lover. He will probably go through the stages of infatuation, attachment, disillusion, and dissolution much faster than you will (after all, he often has more practice in the matter, and more resistance to that chemical rush). In other words, he may be ready to call it quits long before you are.

Yes, it hurts—hell, it stinks! No one wants to be a nonentity, and if you're the single person in an affair, that's often what you revert back to once the married lover has moved on. Maybe you got a little taste of the good life, and now that's gone too. You didn't get marriage, you didn't get a baby or nice home. What you did get is older, and maybe more resentful about the rotten way life is treating you.

But no matter how great the pain, the rejection, and the loss, revenge is not an option (see Rule #19). The momentary satisfaction gleaned from dropping a dime on the bastard to his wife is simply not worth it. Such actions aren't going to bring him back, that's for sure. They may even connect him more strongly to his spouse as they fight the threat that you present. Why give her the satisfaction of knowing that he will always run to her when he's in trouble?

Sure, the uninvolved spouse is pretty much a nonentity during the affair, but in reality she *is* a person, the person who got there first. Frankly, you have a lot more in common with her than you might think—you both want more from the man than he's willing, or able, to give. In the end, he has come up short. Let her deal with it.

Still, sporadic affairs and shadow marriages can be among the most intense and passionate times you'll ever know. Nevertheless, you can never allow yourself to get truly invested in such relationships, or take them personally. Desire ebbs and flows, and love is both cynical and cyclical.

Granted you fit your lover's love map, but so might a hundred other women (and fifty of *them* might have already turned him down). Despite your unique traits, what really makes you different from those ninety-nine others in this context is availability and will-ingness. Don't add gullibility to the list.

Remember—the same chemical reactions that drove your lover to you are eventually going to drive him somewhere else. Affairs are for indulgence, self-gratification, and an ultimately futile need to play out ancient reproductive drives. They are not for the long-term, or for raising children. You will always be second best. To pin your hopes on a married lover is a sure road to disappointment.

Someone once said that flying consists of hours of sheer bore-dom punctuated by moments of sheer terror. Well, marriage is much the same, only the hours stretch out into years and sometimes decades. The occasional infidelity is often nothing more than a blip, exciting and sometimes scary, but inconsequential in the long run. Believe it or not, you're most likely going to end up a blip on your married lover's radar screen.

So enjoy affairs for all the good and happy things they have to offer. Play and have fun with a man who may truly be something spe-cial. But don't build your life around a married lover; you may rest assured that he's not building his around you.

IN CONCLUSION

So Now You Know

You now know the reasons why people like you have affairs, and they are incredibly compelling: better reproductive options and the search for a mate closer to your true ideal who may better serve your evolving needs as you serve theirs, perhaps in loving partnership.

If these are your goals, make it your business to seek them discreetly and thoughtfully, without disrupting your primary social and reproductive relationship (which you may find out was the best thing for you in the long run anyway) until *you* are good and ready. After all, you never know when you might need to sound retreat and head for home—and isn't it good to know it's there?

Sometimes sexual and emotional fidelity is best, and sometimes it isn't. The decision is yours, but make it consciously. Don't let your body drive you to do things that may cause you emotional, physical, and economic anguish down the road.

If you choose to cheat, then go for it, but take care to keep your marriage and your affairs utterly separate. Treat your spouse, lovers, and children with the utmost consideration and tact, and you should have a happy—and satisfying—life.

SUGGESTED READING

Adultery, Louise DeSalvo (Beacon Press, 1999).

Adultery—An Analysis of Love and Betrayal, Annette Lawson (HarperCollins, 1989).

Adultery, The Forgivable Sin, Bonnie Eaker Weil, Ph.D. (Hastings House, 1993)

After the Affair, Janis Abrams Spring (Harper Trade, 1997).

The Alchemy of Love and Lust, Theresa L. Crenshaw, M.D. (Pocket Books, 1996).

Anatomy of an Affair, Norman Victor (Ashley Books, 1980).

Anatomy of Love, Helen Fisher, Ph.D. (Fawcett Columbine Books, 1992).

The Art and Science of Love, Albert Ellis (Lyle Stuart, 1962).

Brain Sex—The Real Differences Between Men and Women, D. Jessel and A. Moir (Lyle Stuart, 1991).

The Civilized Couple's Guide to Extramarital Adventure, Peter H. Wyden (Inc., 1977).

Dumped!, Sally Warren (HarperCollins, 1998).

The Emotional Brain, Joseph LeDoux (Simon & Schuster, 1996).

The Encyclopedia of Sexual Behavior, Albert Abarbanel and Albert Ellis (Hawthorne Books, 1964).

Falling in Love, Ayala Malach Pines (Routledge Press, 1999).

The Good Marriage, Judith Wallerstein (Houghton Mifflin, 1995).

Having Love Affairs, Richard Taylor (Prometheus Books, 1990).

High Infidelity, John McNally (ed.), (William Morrow & Co., 1997).

How to Dump Your Wife, Lee Covington (Fender Publishing, 1994).

Is He Cheating?, Ferne Simone and Sammi Sheen (Berkeley Books, 1998).

Kept Women, Leslie McRay (William Morrow & Co., 1989).

Mistresses, Susan Kedgley and Wendy James (Bobbs Merrill, 1975).

The Moral Animal, Robert Wright (Pantheon Books, 1994).

The Myth of Monogamy, David P. Barash and Judith Lipton (W.H. Freeman & Co., 2001).

A Natural History of Love, Diane Ackerman (Random House, 1994).

The Other Woman—True Stories of Betrayal, Leigh Cato (Longstreet Press, 1996).

Private Lies—Infidelity and the Betrayal of Intimacy, Frank Pittman (W.W. Norton Co., 1989).

The Rules, Ellen Fein and Sherrie Scheneider (Warner Books, 1995).

Secret Lovers, Dr. LuAnn Linquist (Lexington Books, 1989).

The Sexual Brain, Simon LeVay (MIT, 1993).

Sperm Wars—The Science of Sex, Robin Baker, Ph.D. (Basic Books, 1996).

Spying on Your Spouse, Kelly Squires (Citadel Press, 1996).

Stalemates, Marcella Weiner & Bernard Starr (New Horizon Press, 1991).

Triangles—Understanding, Preventing, Surviving an Affair, Lana Staheli, Ph.D. (HarperCollins, 1997).

The Wandering Husband, Hyman Spotnitz & Lucy Freeman (Tower Books, 1990).

Why Men Cheat, Paul Blanchard (Luv Books, 1999).

Why Men Stray/Why Men Stay, Susan Kelley (Adams Media Corp., 1996).

INDEX

ABOUT THE AUTHOR

JUDITH E. BRANDT is a New York City native with advanced degrees in Education and Business Administration. She is an accomplished speaker with extensive marketing experience—skills she currently puts to use on behalf of one of the country's most venerable humor magazines.

Judy divides her time between Los Angeles and Colorado. In her spare time she mountain bikes, skis, tours the bars of the world under the guise of playing rugby, and roots for her beloved New York Yankees and Denver Broncos.